CASE STUDIES IN

CULTURAL ANTHROPOLOGY

SERIES EDITORS

George and Louise Spindler

STANFORD UNIVERSITY

THE BALINESE

THE BALINESE

J. STEPHEN LANSING

University of Southern California

Australia • Canada • Mexico • Singapore • Spain • United Kingdom • United States

for John Christopher Lansing

and

Claudia Lorena Sandoval de Vet

Publisher	Ted Buchholz
Senior Acquisitions Editor	Chris Klein
Editorial Assistant	Linda Wiley
Project Editor	Annelies Schlickenrieder
Production Manager	Jane Tyndall Ponceti
Design	Michele Anderson
Illustrations	Thérèse de Vet
Composition	Graphic Express

Cover Photo A Balinese Topeng dancer portraying a noble king. Photo by J. Stephen Lansing.

ISBN: 0-15-500240-6
Library of Congress Catalog Card Number: 94-77552

Wadsworth/Thomson Learning
10 Davis Drive
Belmont CA 94002-3098
USA

For information about our products, contact us:
Thomson Learning Academic Resource Center
1-800-423-0563
http://www.wadsworth.com

For permission to use material from this text, contact us by
Web: http://www.thomsonrights.com
Fax: 1-800-730-2215
Phone: 1-800-730-2214

For permission to use "Map of Bali" (Figure 2, p. 9) and "The Temples in the Villages of Sukawati" (Figure 10, p. 58) from J. Stephen Lansing, *The Three Worlds of Bali* (1983), the publisher is grateful to Praeger Publishers. The illustration of rice terrace cultivation in Bali on p. 123 was created by Bruce Granquist for Editions Nouveaux-Loisirs, 1995. Permission to reproduce the graphic was generously granted by Gallimard, Paris.

Printed in the United States of America
15 14 13 12 11 10 9

Foreword

These case studies in cultural anthropology are designed for students in beginning and intermediate courses in the social sciences, to bring them insights into the richness and complexity of human life as it is lived in different ways, in different places. The authors are men and women who have lived in the societies they write about and who are professionally trained as observers and interpreters of human behavior. Also, the authors are teachers; in their writing, the needs of the student reader remain foremost. It is our belief that when an understanding of ways of life very different from one's own is gained, abstractions and generalizations about the human condition become meaningful.

The scope and character of the series has changed constantly since we published the first case studies in 1960, in keeping with our intention to represent anthropology as it is. We are concerned with the ways in which human groups and communities are coping with the massive changes wrought in their physical and sociopolitical environments in recent decades. We are also concerned with the ways in which established cultures have solved life's problems. And we want to include representation of the various modes of communication and emphasis that are being formed and reformed as anthropology itself changes.

We think of this series as an instructional series, intended for use in the classroom. We, the editors, have always used case studies in our teaching, whether for beginning students or advanced graduate students. We start with case studies, whether from our own series or from elsewhere, and weave our way into theory, and then turn again to cases. For us, they are the grounding of our discipline.

ABOUT THIS CASE STUDY

Ever since Gregory Bateson and Margaret Mead worked in Bali and their well-known films on dance and trance and the Balinese family as well as their publications appeared, this island with its complex artistic and ceremonious culture has been an anthropological cynosure. Clifford Geertz added to its luster, and a congeries of artists, novelists, journalists, psychiatrists, and intellectuals-at-large, both before and after the Mead-Bateson collaboration, have helped make the image of Bali beguiling, fascinating, perplexing, and marvelously intriguing to almost everyone who can read.

It is not strange that millions of tourists have visited Bali and that it has attracted expatriates of several nationalities. Yet Balinese culture survives, in some ways flourishes. This book is not, however, a case study of the impact of tourism on Balinese culture. It is a study of a culture that has been literate for the last millenium or more, with a complex high court as well as a folk art tradition and an ecologically fine-tuned rice terrace irrigation and cultivation system that has evolved over centuries.

The living arts in Bali—the carvings, gamelan orchestras, shadow plays, intricate daily offerings to the gods, ritual dramas such as that of Rangda and Barong, and the poetry—make Bali so "busy" that famous observers have actually complained about it.

These surface aspects of Balinese culture are well known, but Steve Lansing goes deeper. He describes the "inner compass" of the self and the life of the community as two dimensions of the same process and shows how some dimensions of reality become available only through the poetic imagination. Balinese culture becomes an elaborate allegory, created through centuries of thought, scholarship, experience, rumination, and refined utilization of the poetic imagination. The reader who permits what the author is saying to penetrate the deeper levels of consciousness will never be quite the same again.

Though for some readers of this case study the allegorical complexity and sophistication of Balinese culture will be the most impressive feature, for others the analysis of water temples and their roles in regulating use of irrigation water for terraced rice agriculture will be the most compelling. Particularly interesting will be the conflicts between advocates of the "green revolution" with its new "super rice" varieties, together with pesticides and fertilizers, and the traditional water temple system. The analysis of the conflict and its consequences is original with Lansing and is a major contribution to the ethnography and ethnohistory of Bali. It is also significant to understanding an ecological problem and its sociopolitical relationships symptomatic of much that is happening worldwide in this time of exploding populations and strained resources.

For other readers of this case study the most telling part of the story will be the Dutch takeover of Bali in the nineteenth century and the resistance of the Balinese kings and their people to the Dutch military forces. Whole courts—men, women, and children—walked suicidally into the face of Dutch fire. The European press "explained" such behavior as opium-induced. Lansing describes it from the Balinese viewpoint (and documents) quite differently. Ironically, the Dutch seized control of Bali partly as a means of controlling the opium trade. Bali became a major source of imperial revenue.

Throughout this case study the reader is impressed with Steve Lansing's constant reliance on Balinese sources, both interpersonal and literary, for knowledge and perspective. This is not only appropriate to the best of ethnographic and ethnohistorical principles but gives his writing an authenticity and credibility that could be supplied in no other way.

The Balinese will quickly take its place as one of the most important contributions to the *Case Studies in Cultural Anthropology* series. It is good news for those of us who teach introductory anthropology as well as for those of us who are simply interested in Bali.

ABOUT THE AUTHOR

Steve Lansing was born in Ann Arbor, Michigan, in 1950, to parents who liked to travel. His interest in tropical islands began at the age of ten, when he spent a year in Hawaii with his family. He was educated at Wesleyan University and the University of Michigan and wrote his dissertation at the Institute for Advanced Study in Princeton, New Jersey. Since 1977 he has taught anthropology at the University of Southern California.

Lansing began fieldwork in Bali in 1970, as an undergraduate, and has returned countless times. This is his fourth book about Bali (the others are listed in "Recommended Readings"). In 1979 he and Ira Abrams, an anthropological filmmaker, created an hour-long documentary film, *The Three Worlds of Bali,* about a Balinese ceremony that happens only once in a hundred years. In 1988, he worked with an English anthropological filmmaker, André Singer, to create another anthropological film called *The Goddess and the Computer.* The goddess in the title is Dewi Danu, whom Balinese farmers regard as the deity who brings irrigation water to their fields. The computer belongs to Dr. James Kremer, a systems ecologist who has worked with Lansing since 1987 in a study of the role of Balinese water temples in ecological management. The latest chapter in this story will be shown in a PBS science series called "The Human Quest," airing in 1995.

After years of unsuccessful attempts to convince international development agencies to pay attention to the ecological role of water temples, in 1992 Lansing received support from the United Nations Food and Agriculture Organization and the Advanced Technology Group at Apple Computers, Inc. With Alan Petersen, a computer scientist, he developed a simplified geographic information system called "Watershed," designed to create a two-way communication between traditional farming communities and development planners. He spent seven months helping farmers, extension agents, and temple priests use this system in 1993–94, in a project that is expected to continue.

Lansing has also worked with the Skokomish Indian tribe in western Washington state, creating a video ("People of the River") and a simulation model to assist the tribe in their efforts to persuade policy makers that a healthy river system has intrinsic value.

Lansing is married to his favorite collaborator, a classicist named Thérèse deVet. They have two children, to whom this book is dedicated.

George and Louise Spindler
Series Editors
ETHNOGRAPHICS
P. O. Box 38
Calistoga, CA 94515

ACKNOWLEDGMENTS

My first fieldwork in Bali was made possible by Philip McKean, Jeffrey Butler, Ida Pedanda Made Sidemen, Ida Bagus Ketut Sudiasa, Dr. I Gusti Ngurah Bagus, the College of Social Studies at Wesleyan University, and the Indonesian Institute for the Sciences.

From December 1974 to March 1976 I lived in the village of Sukawati, thanks to the courtesy of Anak Agung Gde Poetra and his family. I am especially grateful to Roy Rappaport, Joseph Jorgensen, Aram Yengoyan, Alton Becker, Clifford Geertz, Andrew Toth, Richard Wallis, Mary Zurbuchen, Mark Poffenberger, Ida Bagus Beretha, I Made Sangga, Ketut Madre, Wayan Loceng, Wayan Narta, Nengah Medra, and members of the Faculty of Letters of Udayana University for invaluable assistance during this period of fieldwork.

Filming the Eka Dasa Rudra ceremony in 1979 was made possible by Ira Abrams, Barbara Myerhoff, Alexander Moore, Andrei Simic, Kristina Melcher, and many people in Bali.

I am grateful to the National Science Foundation for supporting my investigations of Balinese water temple networks beginning in 1983, often with the collaboration of systems ecologist James Kremer. Kevin Arrigo and Tyde Richards were instrumental in different ways in creating a computer model of the water temple system. Thanks to André Singer, there is now a documentary film about this research *The Goddess and the Computer.* Data for simulation modeling was obtained with the help of four students from Udayana University: I Gde Suarja, Ni Made Sri Tutik Andhayani, Dewa Gde Adi Parwata, and I Made Cakranegara. Several of their professors at Udayana have helped with both practical and theoretical issues, especially Nyoman Sutawan, Wayan Ardika, Nyoman Netera, and Gusti Ngurah Bagus.

In 1992 Everett Rogers introduced me to Ronny Adhikarya of the United Nations Food and Agriculture Organization, who created a pilot project to test our computer-assisted ecological monitoring ideas in Bali, with the help of Soedradjaat Martaamidjaja of the Indonesian Ministry of Agriculture. Tyde Richards persuaded the Apple computer company to provide computers for the Farmer's Information Center and the staff of the water temple Pura Ulun Danu Batur for this project. Chapter 4 of this book also reflects the contributions of Alit Artha Wiguna, Gusti Nyoman Aryawan, Engkus, Jelantik Sushila, Ir. Sudarto, Cokorde Raka, and Nyoman Widiatmikawati in data gathering and analysis. Thanks also to Michael Scott Rohan, whose science fiction novel about our project (*The Gates of Noan,* Avon Books, 1992) has provided much amusement.

A special debt of gratitude is owed to A. A. Made Djelantik and to several members of the staff of the temple Pura Ulun Danu Batur: the Jero Gde Mekalihan, Guru Nengah Tekah, Guru Badung, the Jero Penyarikan, and Kaki Jewati. Gary Seaman and Patsy Asch helped me find ways to tell my stories, and John Miller, Chris Langton, Walter Fontana, and Charles Taylor showed me new ways to think about temple networks. Christopher Boehm made many helpful suggestions for this book.

I am grateful to the Koninklijk Instituut voor Taal-, Land- en Volkenkunde for permission to publish several historical photographs. Portions of Chapters 4 and 5 are excerpted from two previous publications: *Priests and Programmers: Technologies of Power in the Engineered Landscape of Bali* (Princeton University Press, 1991) and "Emergent Properties of Balinese Water Temples: Coadaptation on a Rugged Fitness Landscape," (*American Anthropologist, 95*(1), 97–114, March 1993).

Finally, my greatest debt is to my wife Thérèse de Vet, whose many roles have included co-investigator, sound recordist, editor, medic, archivist, Dutch translator, and creator of the illustrations for this book.

List of Figures

Contents

1 / Four Questions, Four Journeys

For almost a hundred years, anthropologists have tended to follow a standard format in writing about the peoples they studied. These books generally begin with maps of the field site and notes on history and geography, and then move chapter by chapter from environment and ecology to kinship and social organization, and on to myth, religion, and worldview. Often there is also a concluding chapter about the effects of Western contact. This style of writing grew out of the way nineteenth-century explorers and naturalists wrote about their discoveries: a chapter on the local birds, another on flowers, and one on the local tribes. There are advantages to this kind of organization: each monograph is like an extended entry in an encyclopedia, making it easy to find your way around and extract information. But such books are usually not a lot of fun to read.[1] This book is written in a different style. Rather than presenting you with a short encyclopedia of Balinese culture, I invite you to join me in exploring the questions that interested me in four separate periods of research.

In the winter of 1970, when I was a sophomore in college, Columbia University Press sent out advertisements announcing that they were about to publish a book called *Traditional Balinese Culture*. The book was expensive, but I had just taken an English course on Moby Dick, and the advertisements for the book made Bali sound a lot like Omoo, the imaginary island paradise where Herman Melville jumped ship. So I ordered a copy, and when it came it seemed even better than Omoo (which got a little tedious at times, at least as described by Melville). The book was made up of essays by artists and anthropologists who had lived in Bali in the 1930s. I was particularly attracted by the writings of Katharane Mershon, a dancer from California who stopped in Bali in 1930 on a world cruise and decided not to leave. She built a house near the beach and apprenticed herself to a young Balinese high priest, who agreed to teach her about Balinese religion. Mershon was one of several artists who managed to live in Bali despite the disapproval of the Dutch colonial authorities who governed Bali, and left only when the beginning of World War II forced foreigners to leave the Indies.

After I finished the book, I learned that there was an Indonesian student at my college studying music. A friend introduced us, and she began to give me lessons in Indonesian, which as she explained was not the real language of the Balinese but a trade language that would help me if I ever got to Bali. For by then I was determined to find out whether the world described in the book really existed. But in the winter of 1970 I was an undergraduate with no relevant background in anything relating to anthropology, Bali, or Indonesia. What little I knew about anthropology was not very encouraging: my friends who had taken courses said it was mostly about the violent behavior of primitive people, or the sort of long-winded descriptions of local customs that you tended to skip over in Melville.

David McAllester, an anthropologist on the faculty at my college, came to my rescue by agreeing to supervise a tutorial on the anthropology of Bali as a substitute for the general introductory course. Under David's direction I read *Balinese Character* by Margaret Mead and her then-husband Gregory Bateson, and Bateson's essay on "Bali: The Value System of a Steady State." These were written when Mead and Bateson were both at the beginning of their amazing careers (they were married on the boat that took them to Bali), and opened my eyes to the idea that people's personalities are shaped by their cultures. Mead and Bateson's main point was that the child rearing customs of the Balinese strongly influenced the ways Balinese children came to see the world. This idea was illustrated by hundreds of fascinating photographs showing scenes of daily life, especially the interaction between mothers and children. After Mead and Bateson, I read Clifford Geertz's little monograph on *Person, Time and Conduct in Bali.* Geertz was another famous anthropologist, and a much more recent visitor to Bali, who claimed that the Balinese experienced time as "cyclical" rather than "linear." Reading Geertz, I got the impression that the Balinese treated one another almost like characters in a Eugene O'Neil play. I wasn't completely convinced, but it was encouraging that the anthropologists were just as fascinated by Bali as the artists.

In March 1971 the College of Social Studies at Wesleyan University agreed to send me to Bali, to do research that could lead to an honors thesis in anthropology. Philip McKean, an anthropologist who was then working in Bali, had written to my advisers offering to look after me. So one winter day, I caught a plane from Hartford to Los Angeles, and onward to Hong Kong, Singapore, and finally Jakarta, the capital of Indonesia. It took another week in Jakarta to get all the necessary permits from the Indonesian government to live and study in a Balinese village. But the day finally came when all my papers were in order, and I caught one last airplane flight to Bali. Phil McKean collected me at the airport in a borrowed Russian jeep, and for the next few days Phil gave me an introduction to the life of an anthropologist in a Balinese village. Phil was interested in the effects of tourism on Balinese culture. An airport big enough for jets had been built in Bali two years earlier, and by 1971 the first waves of mass tourism were beginning to wash over Bali. How would the Balinese cope?

Phil had lots to show me, but I was eager to strike out on my own. I had an idea that I was going to pick up where *Traditional Balinese Culture* had left off. So after a few days of Phil's hospitality I moved to a little bungalow in the seaside village of Sanur, where Katharane Mershon had lived in the thirties. Ida Pedanda Made Sidemen, the high priest who was the subject of Mershon's book, was still alive and had become one of the most distinguished Balinese scholar-priests. But while I was welcomed into his household, ready to pick up where Mershon left off, there remained the minor problem of communication. The few hundred words of Indonesian I had managed to learn made for very short conversations.

Within a day or two, however, the priest's family came up with a solution. A nephew of the high priest named Ida Bagus Sastrawan had already worked as an assistant to a French anthropologist, and the word was passed that he would be happy to help me.[2] It seemed like the perfect solution, except that my French was not much better than my Indonesian. And even if I could get by in French, I was a little uneasy about laying out a program of "anthropological research" to a Balinese Brahmin accustomed to working with a real French anthropologist. In truth, I was beginning to feel like a bit of a fraud. I took refuge in my parting gift from David McAllester, something called the *Sussex Manual of Field Anthropology,* which included simple step-by-step instructions, such as "Find an informant . . . Map the village . . . Do a household survey." So with the help of Ida Bagus I started drawing maps, which did not overtax my linguistic skills, and I began to spend a lot of time at the beach.

Sanur is located near a magnificent coral reef, and one of the daily occupations of people in my adopted household was to go fishing. I had brought along a speargun, and I began to make frequent trips to the reef to go spearfishing with one of the younger sons of the household. But as the days passed, I began to feel increasingly uneasy about the anthropology I was supposed to be doing. I confessed as much to Phil McKean. Instead of lecturing me, however, Phil cheered me up by explaining what "fieldwork" means to an anthropologist. Most anthropologists, apparently, did not enter their field site with a good working knowledge of the local language. In many cases the local language is pretty obscure, and the best way to learn it is to go where it is spoken, live with the local people, and gradually pick it up. So apparently going spearfishing and talking to people was a decent start for my "fieldwork," provided I kept a notebook to record my impressions, and did my best to pick up the language as quickly as possible.

Meanwhile, I was doing my best to learn how to sit, stand, walk, enter a room, ask a question, and eat a meal without provoking suppressed giggles from any

Ancient royal bathing pools, still in use

children who happened to be watching. Eating, apparently, was considered to be a rather obscene or animalistic act and was usually done in private, or at least with one's face averted. Bathing, on the other hand, was something most people did in the late afternoon in public fountains or streams, with little regard for privacy. Most people wore sarongs, and older women covered their breasts only in the presence of strangers. But the first day I got up the courage to put on a sarong instead of my trousers, even the adults couldn't suppress their laughter. I was ready to pack my bags until someone explained to me that I had tied the sarong on the side, as women do, rather than in front like a man. Years later, I was reminded of this incident the first time I took my eight-year-old daughter to a tourist beach, after we'd been living for months in a mountain village. Claudia had exactly the same reaction as the Balinese children: the sight of all those foreigners on the beach with their sarongs tied every which way sent her into fits of giggles. But that was much later. When I left Bali in August of 1971, I had enough notes to turn into a senior thesis.[3] More importantly, I knew that I wanted to return as a real anthropologist.

After three more years in the classroom, I fled another chilly university campus and returned to Bali for a year and a half to do the research for my doctoral dissertation in anthropology. My official topic was the role of art in Balinese society, and once again I was a little surprised that I was able to get away with it. I kept expecting my professors to redirect me towards something more serious, like kinship or archaeology. But the question was a good one, even if it did sound suspiciously like too much fun. Anthropologists had not written very much about the cross-cultural study of art, and most studies were framed in terms of a supposed contrast between "Great Traditions" (the art of the elite); "Little," "Folk," or "Popular Traditions" (the art of everyday people); and "Primitive" or "Tribal Art" (which might or might not include the Balinese). But from what I had seen in 1971, it seemed to me that this classification system completely missed the mark in Bali. Painting, sculpture, music, architecture, poetry—all of the arts Western philosophers classify as "Fine Arts"— were part of everyday life for ordinary people in Bali. And I was not the first visitor to make this observation. The great silent-movie comedian Charlie Chaplin visited Bali in the thirties with the English playwright Noel Coward. Before they left, Coward wrote the following "complaint" in the comments section of his hotel register:

As I said this morning to Charlie
There is far too much music in Bali
And although as a place it's entrancing
There is also a thought too much dancing
It appears that each Balinese native
From the womb to the tomb is creative
And although the results are quite clever
There is too much artistic endeavor![4]

Coward meant to be funny, of course (though the joke was not discovered for years), but even serious anthropologists like Margaret Mead were impressed by the importance of the arts in Balinese life. In 1937 Mead returned to New York after two years of fieldwork in a Balinese village. In one of her first publications about Bali she described how the Balinese consume their agricultural surplus in complicated ways:

Here was an almost incredible busyness; day and night, the roads were full of people walking with a light and swinging step under heavy loads; the air was never empty of music, even in the small hours before the dawn, and it was not mere woodland piping but complicated orchestral music that bore witness to many hours of concentrated rehearsal . . . their lives were packed with intricate and formal delights.[5]

By the time I got to Bali, several good books about art had already been written. Colin McPhee, an American composer, published a wonderful book about his experience of Balinese music called *A House in Bali*. And Walter Spies, a German painter, teamed up with an American writer to produce *Dance and Drama in Bali*. I saw no need to add another tribute to the creative genius of the Balinese. But I did wonder what the Balinese themselves might have to say about the meaning of art in their culture. How did they talk about art? Why were some Balinese villages specialized in particular art forms, like painting or sculpture or the crafting of musical instruments? Was knowledge of the arts limited to particular groups?

In pursuit of answers to these questions, I decided in the fall of 1974 to move into a couple of rooms in the old ruined palace of Sukawati, one of the major centers of artistic innovations over the past century. The village of Sukawati was formerly the capital of a small princedom attached to the royal court of Gianyar in central Bali. The old palace had been mostly destroyed by cannon fire in a nineteenth-century battle, but many impoverished descendants of the princely family continued to live in and around the old palace. More importantly for my purposes, Sukawati was still a major center for many of the arts. Walking through the village on almost any afternoon I could hear the sound of people practicing music for the gamelan orchestra, and just behind the palace walls there was a whole row of houses belonging to storytellers, musicians, and puppeteers. Not far away was a cluster of houses belonging to members of the wood-and-stone-carver's descent group.

Living in Sukawati meant that I would not see much of my old friends in Sanur. But Sanur was rapidly becoming a center of tourism, and my friends there agreed that Sukawati was a much better place to investigate the role of art in a traditional setting. With Sukawati as my base, and a clunky old British motorcycle, I traveled around the island comparing the role of the arts in different villages and principalities. Chapter 3 of this book is mostly based on that fieldwork. But while I learned enough to write a dissertation about art and society in Bali, I also got sidetracked.

The period 1974–76, when I was studying the role of the arts, was a time of tremendous change in Bali and in much of Asia, caused by a process that goes by the name of the "Green Revolution." The name refers to the introduction of new hybrid varieties of food crops like wheat, rice, and potatoes to developing countries like Indonesia (of which Bali is a province). Beginning in the 1960s, many governments set up crash programs to spread the Green Revolution, as quickly as possible, to ensure that their food supply would not lag behind the needs of a growing population. The Green Revolution reached Bali in the 1970s, causing a rapid increase in rice production. But by the mid-1970s some of these gains were being offset by ecological disasters: explosions of rice pests and breakdowns in the irrigation systems. While all this was going on, I was spending a lot of time visiting Balinese temples, since most artistic performances are held during temple festivals. Many Balinese temples are connected with agricultural gods and goddesses and, as I listened to farmers talking in these temples, I

An array of flower offerings to the gods

began to realize that the role of the temples was undergoing a profound change. Apparently some of the temples played an important practical role in scheduling water use and cropping patterns for whole farming districts. But as a result of the Green Revolution, the temples were forbidden to carry out these functions. Instead, every farmer was urged to plant rice as often as possible. As a result, the traditional system of collective management of water resources was coming apart. The more I learned about these agricultural temples, the more interested I became in their ecological role, and in the enormous body of "traditional" knowledge possessed by farmers and temple priests about managing the ecology of the rice terraces. So while I was carrying out my research on the arts, I also began to pay attention to the ecological role of the water temples. The subject was too vast for me to make much progress at that time, but I learned enough to become convinced that this would be a fascinating topic for future research. Soon afterwards the ecological effects of the Green Revolution became the main focus of a new research project, which I'll talk about in Chapter 4.

In 1977, I got a job as an assistant professor of anthropology. Meanwhile, the Balinese were preparing for a very important event: the year 1979 on our calendar would mark the beginning of a new century on the Balinese calendar, which they planned to mark with the greatest religious ceremony in the history of Bali, a grand island-wide ritual of purification and world renewal called Eka Dasa Rudra. I was naturally dying to be there, but the ceremony was scheduled for March—the middle of the semester—and I didn't see how I could manage to get away. But my friend and colleague Ira Abrams, an anthropological filmmaker, came up with a wonderful plan. He suggested that we make a documentary film about the ceremony for a new anthropology series on public television called "Odyssey." Ira talked "Odyssey" into taking a gamble on us, and in March 1979 we flew to Bali with a crew consisting of a camera operator, sound recordist, two students, and a ton of equipment. A few weeks later we returned to campus with fourteen hours of film footage that we edited into a one-hour film for "Odyssey" called *The Three Worlds of Bali*. Chapter 5 of this book is partly about the meaning of this ceremony and others like it.

Chapter 5 takes up several other topics besides the world-renewal ceremonies, all having to do with what anthropologists call the "ethnohistory" of Bali. I have placed this chapter at the end of the book, instead of the beginning, because I think that the most interesting questions about Balinese history only come into focus when the reader has some background in Balinese culture. As a matter of fact, much of Balinese history was nearly lost for good, buried beneath the histories written by foreigners. These scholars did not deliberately distort the historical record. But lacking an open-ended anthropological view of Balinese culture, they tended to find only what they were looking for.

The last part of Chapter 5 brings us to the present, focusing on the effects of tourism and development on modern Bali. In the past twenty years, Bali has become one of the most popular destinations for tourists in Asia, with a large international airport and hundreds of hotels. While tourism was never a subject of my research, in one way or another it affected most of the subjects I was interested in. Tourists provided a new market for many of the arts, for example, while the creation of tourist hotels and businesses influenced the farm economy. But I suspect you'll find all this

Figure 1   Map of Indonesia

more interesting when you know something about the traditional Balinese way of
life, the subject that first drew me to Bali.

THE GEOGRAPHY AND PREHISTORY OF BALI

For years I have admired the way John McPhee writes about geography, in books like
Basin and Range, Rising from the Plains, and *The Control of Nature.* In McPhee's
books, simple descriptions gradually turn into the pieces of a puzzle that becomes
ever more intriguing as its dimensions expand. While a McPhee-style analysis of the
geography of Bali would be fascinating, we haven't the space for it here. But it's time
you got acquainted with the island, so I'll try to set the Balinese geographical stage
with a few quick strokes.

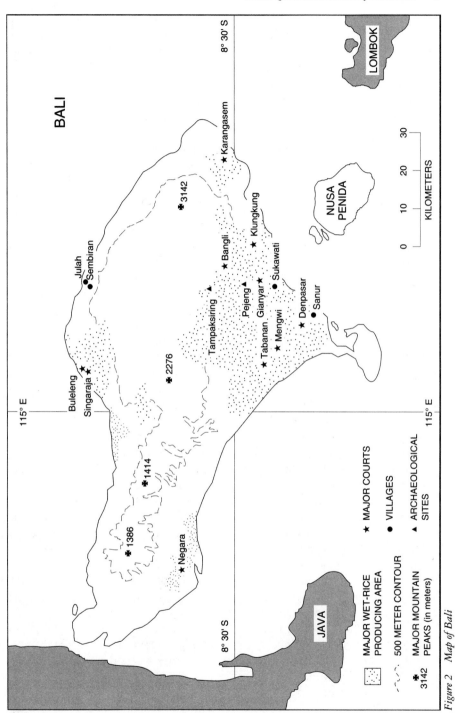

Figure 2   Map of Bali

The southern arc of islands of the Indonesian archipelago is part of the Ring of Fire, a chain of active volcanoes marking the intersection of two tectonic plates. Bali lies near the midpoint of the arc, separated by only a few kilometers of ocean from its island neighbor to the west (Java), and by a wider and rougher channel to the east. Standing on the summit of a Balinese volcano, on a clear day you can see an apparently endless range of volcanic peaks stretching away to the eastern and western horizons. But clear days are rare, because Bali lies just south of the Equator, in the region of tropical monsoons. Each year, several hundred inches of rain fall on most of the island. Looking down from the summit of a volcano towards the seacoast, the effects of this rainfall on Bali's fertile soils are apparent in the dense tropical forests. Until about a thousand years ago, when the Balinese developed irrigation technology, these forests covered most of the island. But today they survive only at high elevations and in the western third of the island, which lacks suitable conditions for irrigation and is mostly uninhabited. The western forest was wild enough to provide a habitat for tigers until early in this century, when they were hunted to extinction by Europeans. Today several rare species of birds such as Rothschild's mynah are found only in this region. The northeastern tip of the island is also sparsely populated, but for a different reason: it lies in a rain shadow and has very little water, the few streams mostly flowing only during the rainy season.

The vast majority of Balinese live in a south-facing natural amphitheater created by the curving chain of volcanoes that form the geological backbone of the island. The dimensions are small: from the eastern border of the Balinese rice bowl to the western is about fifty miles, and from the uppermost rice terraces to the sea is never more than twenty-five miles. The landscape is constantly being rearranged by volcanic eruptions, which deposit large quantities of ash over whole districts while burying others under lava flows. The natural ruggedness of the volcanic landscape is further enhanced by the streams and rivers rushing down the sides of the mountains. The torrential rains that fall in the rainy season and the steepness of the slopes combine to give these rivers a sharp cutting edge on the soft volcanic rock. There are about eighty rivers in the southern rice bowl, and most of them have sliced channels fifty to two hundred feet below the surface of the surrounding landscape. The sides of the ravines are often so steep that it is nearly impossible to climb down one side and up the other, making lateral (east–west) travel a difficult proposition unless one finds a bridge. Traveling along the north–south axis is usually much easier, even though it involves climbing or descending the slopes of the volcanoes.

Within this region—the southern rice bowl of Bali—for more than a thousand years, generations of farmers have gradually transformed the landscape, clearing forests, digging irrigation canals, and terracing hillsides to enable themselves and their descendants to grow irrigated rice. As the rice terraces expanded and the population grew, villages were probably forced to migrate from the valleys to the hillsides, and eventually all the way up to the ridge tops where the irrigation canals could not reach. Today most villages are strung almost end-to-end along the ridgelines running down the slopes of the volcanoes. The rest of the landscape is almost entirely given over to the rice terraces. If you fly over Bali in the late summer when the terraces are flooded after the first rice harvest, on a sunny day the landscape is a dazzling shattered mirror of reflections from the rice paddies, framed by the winding green lines of forested ridges climbing down the mountains. A few months later, the water in the terraces is hidden beneath soft green carpets of rice sweeping down the valleys to the sea.

On the other side of the mountains, the northern coastline of Bali presents a similar picture of villages and agricultural lands, but on a smaller scale. In 1876, a Dutch colonial officer saw the northern rivers as "strips of silver in the green mountains." Most of the northern rivers support only one or two villages, which are usually situated just above the narrow coastal plain. Further inland, the mountains are too steep to support traditional forms of agriculture, although in the modern era these areas are often planted with coffee, vanilla, and other commercial crops. There are ancient paths through the mountains linking the northern and southern villages. While the south has the best agricultural land, the best trade routes are via the northern coast, which has been involved in sea trade since prehistoric times. Even today, the seas to the south of Bali are usually empty of shipping, while those to the north are a busy commercial highway.

The study of the prehistoric settlement of Bali has only recently begun, and there are still many unanswered questions. Dutch archaeologists of the colonial era (1849–1942) tended to interpret their findings in terms of a continuous sequence of human occupation stretching back into the distant past. Bali is one of the stepping-stones in the land bridge that once connected the islands of Indonesia to the Asian mainland, and we now know that the earliest inhabitants of Australia and New Guinea crossed this bridge at least fifty thousand years ago. But the assumption that the ancestors of the Balinese had lived in the region for tens of thousands of years has proven to be quite wrong.

Archaeologists have discovered convincing evidence that the ancestors of the modern Balinese arrived by sea from the north about four or five thousand years ago. They were probably met by representatives of an even earlier human population. But as yet we know almost nothing about Bali's original inhabitants, whereas we know a great deal about the ancestors of the present-day Balinese. Most scholars trace their origins to the island of Taiwan (Formosa) about six thousand years ago, to a group of people known to prehistorians as the Austronesians. Between 3000 B.C. and A.D. 400, the Austronesians colonized most of the inhabitable islands of the Pacific, from the Philippines to Hawaii and Easter Island. They also settled on the coasts of Malaysia, southern Vietnam, and even the island of Madagascar, off the east coast of Africa. Archaeologists have long been interested in the question of what led the Austronesians to undertake these extraordinary long-distance voyages, which spread their language and culture over nearly half the surface of the earth.[6]

The evidence needed to answer this question is now beginning to appear. The island of Taiwan lies off the east coast of China. During the Upper Pleistocene it was connected to China by a land bridge, but with the end of the Ice Age the sea level rose and Taiwan became an island, with a small human population supporting themselves by hunting and gathering. Around eight thousand years ago, food crops like rice and millet were domesticated on the Chinese mainland, beginning the Neolithic revolution in China (the transition from hunting and gathering to horticulture and settled village life). Neolithic technology quickly spread to China's southern coast, and it appears that some colonists brought this agricultural way of life across the sea to Taiwan about six thousand years ago. They spoke a language linguists call Proto-Austronesian, and the spread of this language is one of the most useful kinds of evidence for tracing the movements of the Austronesians. Some Proto-Austronesian speakers ventured southwards to the northern Philippines by about 3000 B.C., probably in search of new land, or perhaps to take advantage of new resources discovered by fishermen.

We know quite a lot about their culture, thanks to a combination of linguistic and archaeological data. The Austronesians were farmers and fishermen, who domesticated pigs, chickens, and dogs and grew rice, millet, and sugarcane. Later, their descendants added taro, breadfruit, coconut, banana, yam, and sago. They built seagoing canoes and fished with hooks, nets, and Derris poison. They lived in villages, worshipped a pantheon of nature gods and ancestors, and built temples to their gods in the form of rectangular stone-walled courtyards. Temples of this type are found on many of the islands of the Pacific, and prehistoric remains of similar structures have been found in many parts of Bali, although none of them have yet been excavated by archaeologists.

While most of the descendants of the Malayo-Polynesians continued their seafaring traditions in the Pacific, the Balinese gradually turned inwards, exploiting the fertility of their magnificent island. Eventually, the ancestors of the Balinese developed metalworking, irrigation systems, literacy, and many other innovations that made Bali increasingly unlike most other Pacific island societies. Archaeologists began to piece together the story of Balinese prehistory in the 1920s.

In 1921, the Dutch scholar P. de Kat Angelino found a small stone sarcophagus in a mountain temple in Bali. Later, many more sarcophagi were found, some still containing human skeletons and burial goods, such as bronze ornaments and beads made of glass and carnelian. Most of the 115 stone sarcophagi now identified were found near the Pakerisan and Petanu rivers in south Bali. They vary in size from small (80–120 cm) to large (200–268 cm), and in weight from 200 to 1,200 kilograms. Metal objects discovered in sarcophagus burials include bronze finger and arm protectors, double-spiral wire necklaces, earrings, belts, chest protectors, crescent-bladed socketed axes, and gold eye-covers. The presence of these valuable objects suggests that the sarcophagi were used for the burial of members of an elite. This implies that social stratification (the emergence of chiefdoms) occurred in Bali during the Early Metal period, in the first millenium A.D. or perhaps even earlier.

An even more significant discovery was made by K.C. Crucq in 1932. In the village of Manuaba, Crucq found fragments from a stone mold used to cast bronze kettledrums (*moko*). The existence of these drums had long been known, but the discovery of the casting mold provided evidence that these metal objects were actually manufactured in Bali, not imported from somewhere else. This discovery had further implications: bronze is made from tin and copper, neither of which are found on Bali. The high percentages of tin and lead in the Balinese drums, as well as their complex ornamentation, indicate a relatively advanced prehistoric technology of metalworking. Moreover, kettledrums closely resembling the ones made in Manuaba have been found on many islands to the east of Bali. Thus the discovery of the bronze casting molds provided evidence for the existence of an interisland trading system in prehistoric times, by means of which copper and tin were brought to Bali, and finished bronze artifacts were traded to the eastern archipelago.

Two Balinese stone sarcophagi. Date: Late Formative, circa *early first millenium c.e. National Museum of Archaeology, Pejeng, Bali.*

Recently, a Balinese archaeologist (Dr. I Wayan Ardika) has begun systematic excavations at several sites along the northern coast, and his findings illuminate the key transition from prehistoric tribal communities to literate kingdoms. One of the most intriguing questions in the prehistory of Bali is the origin of the irrigated rice-terrace system that provided the economic foundation of later Balinese kingdoms. Ardika believes that the invention of irrigation was probably a major factor in the origin of the Balinese state. In Bali, the story of the development of irrigation technology is linked to the question of the beginnings of rice cultivation, because irrigation is used primarily to grow rice in paddy fields. But when did the Balinese first begin to grow rice?

In 1992, Ardika found rice husks at a depth of 3.5 meters in an excavation at the village of Sembiran, along the coast of north Bali. Specimens of the rice were radiocarbon dated, with a date of 2660 ± 100 B.P. (In other words, the rice is approximately 2,660 years old).[7] This is probably a thousand years before the invention of irrigation technology, implying that at first rice was grown using natural rainfall or in swampy areas. The building of irrigation canals in Bali undoubtedly required the use of metal tools to carve tunnels through the soft volcanic rock, since, as we noted before, most Balinese rivers are found at the bottom of deep ravines, making it necessary for farmers to build tunnels to obtain water for irrigation. So the archaeological evidence suggests that rice came first, followed by the development of metal tools in the early first millenium, and the beginnings of irrigation. The earliest direct evidence for irrigation technology comes from royal inscriptions of the ninth century A.D., which refer to irrigation tunnel builders.[8]

Some of the earliest known sculptures showing Indian influence on the Balinese arts. These figures may be images of Hindu gods, or Balinese kings and queens. Gunung Penulisan, Bali.

But when did literate kingdoms first appear on Bali? And—since the first Balinese kingdoms were modeled on Indian examples—what was the nature of Indian influence in the transition from chiefdoms to kingdoms? Several early inscriptions from the north coast of Bali refer to trade with foreigners, and Ardika wondered whether evidence of such trade could be discovered by an archaeological excavation. He decided to dig where the inscriptions indicated that a trading community existed in the ninth century A.D.

His very first excavations were rewarded by the discovery of Indian artifacts: Indian rouletted ware pottery along with glass beads. The pottery was analyzed with X-ray diffraction and dated to between the late first century B.C. and about A.D. 200. These dates led to a new puzzle: they are over half a millenium older than the first written inscriptions on Bali. Was there continuous trade with foreign civilizations for five hundred years before the Balinese developed kingdoms of their own? Or did kingship originate much earlier than the first inscriptions we know about?

Here is a possible scenario for the emergence of the first Balinese kingdom. The spring of Tirtha Empul in south-central Bali (mentioned in the quotation from Stutterheim) pours out around seven hundred liters of water per second. Today, that water is channeled down the valley to irrigate several hundred hectares of rice terraces, which are located in the region of Pejeng. Pejeng happens to be situated at the center of the distribution of archaeological remains, like stone sarcophagi, copper-plate inscriptions, and ancient buildings, such as monasteries and tombs. Nearly everywhere else in Bali, to get water for irrigation it is necessary to dig tunnels and canals, but the water from the spring at Tirtha Empul flows freely down the valley. To me, the evidence suggests that this was the site of the earliest irrigation system in Bali, and the first kingdom. We know that the Balinese were already growing rice in prehistoric times, probably in swampy areas along the coast. Channeling the water from the spring would enable farmers to grow irrigated rice, which is a great deal more productive and can support many more people. It is hard for me to imagine irrigation starting out in Bali with underground tunnels. But I can easily imagine farmers channeling the spring water from Tirtha Empul to construct the first rice terraces in the valley just north of Pejeng. Later, after the valley filled up and the farmers needed more water for irrigation, it would be sensible for them to start damming rivers and digging tunnels a little farther afield. Recently I've begun to work with Ardika and a young American archaelogist, John Schoenfelder, to gather the evidence needed to test this hypothesis.

The appearance of the first kingdom and the adoption of writing mark the end of the prehistoric era in Bali, and the beginnings of written history. I will not pursue the story of Balinese history any further here (we will return to this subject in Chapter 5). Instead, now that we have some background on the geography and prehistory of Bali, we will proceed directly to an account of fieldwork in a Balinese village.

NOTES

1. The eminent French anthropologist Dan Sperber writes: "The culture under study is displayed in the form of a continuous and homogeneous discourse, neither too concrete, nor too abstract, and organized in chapters of equal length. Works of the same school often have the same table of contents, in order, no doubt, to pave the way for the work of comparison, which is always planned but rarely undertaken. With few exceptions, to read these writings requires a commendable perseverance." Dan Sperber, *On Anthropological Knowledge.* Cambridge University Press, 1985:6.

2. Louis Berthes

3. Later published as *Evil in the Morning of the World: Phenomenological Approaches to a Balinese Community.* Ann Arbor: Michigan Papers on South and Southeast Asia No. 6, 1974.

4. Quoted in Frank Clune, *To the Isles of Spice.* Sydney: Angus and Robertson, 1940:317.

5. Margaret Mead, "The Arts in Bali," originally published in *The Yale Review,* Vol. XXX, No. 2 (December 1940):333; reprinted in Jane Belo, ed., *Traditional Balinese Culture.* New York: Columbia University Press, 1970.

6. For a clear account of the prehistoric voyages of the Malayo-Polynesians, see Peter Bellwood, "The Austronesian Dispersal and the Origin of Languages," *Scientific American,* Vol. 265, No. 1 (July 1991):88–93, or Bellwood's book *Prehistory of the Indo-Malaysian Archipelago.* New York: Academic Press, 1985.

7. I Wayan Ardika, "The discovery of rice (oryza sativa) in the trenches of Sembiran and Pacung," Majalah Ilmiah Universitas Udayana, Vol. XIX, No. 34 (October 1992):1.

8. For example, an inscription dated 818 Icaka refers to undagi pangarung (irrigation tunnel builders). See Roelof Goris, Prasasti Bali 1. Bandung: N.V. Masa Baru, 1954:55.

2 / Beginning Fieldwork

INTRODUCTION

My fieldwork began in the village of Sanur, on the south coast of Bali. In 1906, the Dutch colonialists stationed warships off the coast at Sanur and rained explosive projectiles on the interior, in an unequal contest that ended with the death of the last Balinese king. It's a good story, and we'll get to it eventually. But in March 1971, Sanur was a peaceful place, famous among Europeans for the new luxury hotel on its beach, and among Balinese as a center of witchcraft.

I was introduced to Sanur by Phil McKean, an American anthropologist who was working in a nearby village. Most anthropologists have to start their fieldwork from scratch by building up relationships with the people they hope to study, but thanks to Phil's help I was able to take a shortcut. Many older people in Sanur still remembered Katharane Mershon, the American dancer who lived there before World War II and wrote a book about the famous Brahmin priest Pedanda Made. Phil sent word to Pedanda Made that he was expecting a visit from an American student who wanted to meet him. A few days later a message came back that the priest's family was willing to help me.

So one morning a few days after my arrival in Bali I moved into a little house in Sanur. The house was a kind of Balinese interpretation of a tiny Dutch bungalow, built to entertain Western visitors. The interior consisted of a couple of small bare rooms furnished with Dutch cupboards, beds, and chairs, with a sitting room opening onto a wide veranda. The bungalow sat in the midst of a flower garden, enclosed by high stone walls on all four sides. Three of the walls had doorways leading off to other courtyards, guarded by ferocious-looking stone sculptures of demons. Early in the morning, two or three little girls showed up with bamboo poles to knock blossoms off the plumeria trees, which they collected in baskets. Later in the day, other women arrived carrying stacks of little offerings made from the flowers, which they casually placed at each of the gates as offerings to unseen spirits.

My bungalow and garden were located deep inside a maze of about thirty similar courtyards containing houses, kitchens, storerooms and temples, all belonging to members of a high-ranking descent group, the Brahmana Mas. Out the north gate, two left turns took me to the entrance gate to the compound belonging to my landlord, the unofficial head of the whole extended Brahman family, who was also the elected head or mayor (*perbekel*) of the village. Out the west gate, across a little street, down an alley, and a left turn into another courtyard brought me to the residence of Pedanda

A girl arranges offerings to the gods in a temple festival.

Made himself, Katharane Mershon's great teacher of the 1930s, now a very old man. And the east gate led into a beautiful temple, a courtyard with many statues and shrines to the gods, generally empty of people except for the occasional visits of little girls bringing small flower offerings and incense to the shrines.

To leave my own courtyard meant that I had to walk along little paths leading between—and in some cases right through—the courtyards of my neighbors. The same was true for my neighbors: throughout the day there was a steady stream of people walking through my garden on their way to see the mayor or other families living in adjacent courtyards. So my first question was how to behave towards these casual visitors, who politely ignored my existence unless I greeted them. I found that if I said "Good morning" in the Indonesian language, they repeated this greeting; while if I tried the standard Balinese salutation, "lunga kija" ("Where are you going?"), they answered rather vaguely in Balinese ("north"; or "to the mayor"; or "just strolling"). It did not take long to figure out that it was good manners to greet people, but not to try to detain them with longer conversations, since they obviously had things to do. The little girls would happily respond to my simple questions, for example, without pausing for a moment in their flower collecting.

My first real conversations were with Ida Bagus Sastrawan, the nephew of the high priest, who had agreed to help me with my research. Soon after I moved in, Ida Bagus appeared on my veranda and we began to experiment with various languages to see which one got us furthest. It embarrasses me a little now to remember how I dashed into the inner room to retrieve my tape recorder, so that I could begin my "fieldwork" by tape-recording our conversation. Naturally the tape recorder jammed, whereupon Ida Bagus gently picked it up, removed the cassette, rewound the tape around its sprocket, and turned the machine on for me, meanwhile asking politely what I intended to record.

The machine soon went back into a cupboard, and I began to spend most of my time with Ida Bagus and his family, watching what went on, trying to pick up the language, and going to the beach once or twice a day. Ida Bagus was in his late forties when I first met him. As the nephew of Pedanda Made and second cousin of the mayor, he was related to the two most important men in the village. But he had inherited neither property nor position. Although he was a devoted student of Balinese sacred literature, Ida Bagus felt that he could not himself aspire to become a high priest, since that position had already been taken by his elder brother. Instead, he and his family supported themselves mostly by making offerings to the gods for rituals such as birthdays, weddings, and temple festivals, which were sold to the families who came to visit his brother, the high priest. Most of the offerings were made from palm fronds, carefully cut and shaped into elaborate designs, into which flower petals and other beautiful things were woven. It was this little industry that was taking such a toll on the flowers in my own courtyard, most of which went into baskets belonging to the daughters and nieces of Ida Bagus.

He himself was seldom involved in the preparation of the offerings, since most of them are traditionally made by women. Instead, he studied sacred manuscripts borrowed from the library of the old priest that contained detailed descriptions of the kinds of offerings required for particular events, in order to make sure that the right offerings were prepared for each client. All this activity was very puzzling to me at

Ida Bagus reading a lontar manuscript

first—what was so important about offerings, and why were there so many?—but in time I understood that Ida Bagus was a sort of lesser priest or part-time ritual specialist, helping clients to carry out the specific rituals prescribed by high priests like his older brother.

But in 1971 most people in Bali were very poor, having suffered through decades of war, inflation, political turmoil, and most recently the economic collapse of the 1960s. Ten years later, the income from the preparation of offerings was enough to support the family, but it wasn't long after I met him that I realized that the little fish he caught most mornings inside the reef were an important part of the family diet. Ida Bagus and his sons did most of their fishing wading in waist-deep water between the reef and the beach, using a little throw-net and a basket. As soon as I began to spearfish on the reef, I began to wonder why he and his fellow fishermen were using such an inefficient technique. They usually returned from a fishing expedition with a handful of minnows, which couldn't compare with the tremendous variety of reef fish I could see—and occasionally spear—while snorkeling over the reef. Like most Balinese but unlike most other Pacific islanders, Ida Bagus did not know how to swim. Here was another puzzle: imagine, a society of people living by a coral reef who are unable to swim! So, like other visitors before me, I became interested in the question of why the Balinese make so little use of their marine resources.

I remembered that several of the authors of articles in *Traditional Balinese Culture* had addressed this question. Jane Belo made an interesting case that the Balinese fear of the ocean was connected to a more general pattern of ideas about space. As Belo put it:

> One learns that the Balinese is never unconscious of his position in space in relation to *kaja,* north, which is the direction of the mountains, and *kelod,* south, the direction of the sea; and in relation to his position above the ground, which should not be higher than that of his social superior. It would seem that a good deal of the "carefulness" in the manner of the Balinese springs from his habit of adjusting his position according to the laws of his cosmology and his social group. . . . Every Balinese sleeps with his head either to the north or the east. He may not even lie down for a moment in the opposite direction, for the feet are dirty and may not be put in the place of the head.[9]

Following up on this question seemed like a good way to begin my fieldwork. If Belo was right, I ought to be able to observe these patterns of behavior for myself. So I stopped drawing maps, and began to pay more attention to what was going on around me.

BEGINNING RESEARCH

It was easy for me to watch what went on in the neighborhood and to participate in family life, because Balinese spend very little time indoors. A Balinese house is really a walled compound containing a collection of buildings, most of which have walls on only two sides. So most of the people in the household are in sight of everyone else except when they are asleep, or eating in the kitchen. Balinese are seldom alone, and people generally like to chat while carrying on their innumerable daily

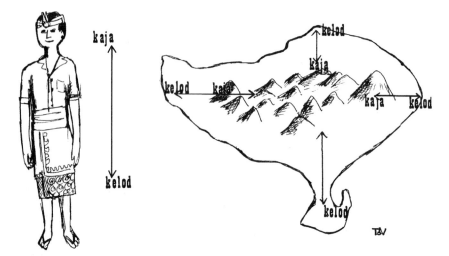

Figure 3   "Kaja" and "kelod." "Kaja" means "upstream" or "towards the summit;" "kelod" means "downstream" or "towards the sea." These directions also may refer to a human body, or any object in space.

tasks. Life seems quite casual, but one quickly learns that everything has its place, and that spatial orientation is crucial for every kind of activity. The layout of buildings and activities in each houseyard reflects the same orientation toward space that makes the ocean a dangerous place. As Belo noted, the direction upstream or towards the mountains in the center of the island is called *kaja* in Balinese, while the direction seawards is called *kelod*. In a similar way, a person's head is kaja, while his feet are kelod. Shrines to the ancestors are located at the kaja corner of a houseyard; kitchens, stock pens, and bathrooms are kelod. It is impolite to touch people on their heads, even children, and one of the problems my neighbor the mayor faced with the foreign employees brought in for the new luxury hotel was their habit of hanging laundry as high as a man's head. The same problem with regard to space also kept the high priest and other religious Brahmans from setting foot inside the new hotel, since by doing so they would place their heads beneath the feet of the people standing on the higher floors of the hotel. With respect to other villages, the whole community of Sanur was kelod (seawards) by virtue of its location at the beach, which helped to explain its reputation as a center of sorcery. Before the arrival of the tourists, the land nearest the beach was often used as a cemetery. This meant that new hotels tended to be located in supernaturally dangerous spots, and there were lots of stories about haunted hotel rooms. The reader may wonder how it could be that foreigners could be given permission to build hotels on cemeteries. The reason is that Balinese bury their dead only temporarily, returning after a period of months or years to exhume the remains for cremation. Cemeteries are therefore only temporary homes for the dead, and one seaside location is just as good as another.

   Yet it would be wrong to conclude that for the Balinese upstream is good and downstream is bad. Houses need stock pens, kitchens, and bathrooms, as well as shrines to the ancestors, and villages need cemeteries. Kaja and kelod are viewed as complementary opposites. They are like a compass needle, pointing to the mountain-top and the sea, and everything in the social world of the Balinese is supposed to harmonize with this directional symbolism. My strongest memories of this first period of fieldwork are about learning how to navigate in a world where spatial orientation had such importance. As an American, I came from a culture where this concept of cosmic symmetry simply didn't exist. It isn't that space is not meaningful in an American household: try mixing up the arrangement of things that "belong" in the garage, bathroom, bedroom, or living room! But in Connecticut, I did not need to sleep with my head pointed toward the sacred mountains, or worry that I might become sick because the doors to my house were oriented in the wrong direction.

DEFINING A RESEARCH TOPIC

Beginning anthropologists are taught to use their own personal experience as fieldworkers to gain insights into the culture they are investigating. This is especially useful advice if you arrive in the field without a well-defined research topic! Fortunately, a few months after I moved into the village—I'm not sure exactly when—I began to realize that there were interesting connections between what I was finding out about spatial symbolism and what Mead and Bateson had written about Balinese concepts of childhood and the human life cycle. When I mentioned this idea to Ida Bagus, he enthusiastically agreed. Apparently, most of the rituals he helped perform made reference to a kind of map of the inner self, which was based on the kaja–kelod axis but also included other spatial directions: four or eight points of the compass, as well as the zenith, nadir, and center. This map could be seen in the ritual offerings made by his wife and daughters, if I would take the trouble to learn the meanings of the colors of the flowers and the patterns in which they were arranged. According to Ida Bagus, understanding this spatial symbolism was the key to most of the questions I was asking, from the layout of the village to the meaning of the rituals performed for babies and small children. Understanding the symbolism of the language of flowers would provide me with a kind of map of the inner world of the self. The same map also referred to the "outer worlds" of the village and the island. And it also had to do with witchcraft. All this sounded fascinating, and by then I was eager to find a research topic that was well enough defined to become the basis for my senior thesis. So we agreed that my topic would be the Balinese map of the inner and outer worlds. Ida Bagus also warned me that this subject was much deeper than I could possibly cover in a few short months, especially in view of my limited language skills. Moreover, some aspects of this knowledge were secret and could not be explained to me even if I were able to understand them. But he said that even a superficial understanding of the inner map would help me begin to see past the surface appearance of things, to the hidden structure of the world.

THE BALINESE MAP OF THE INNER AND OUTER WORLDS

At first, it all seemed quite simple. According to Ida Bagus, the cosmos is divided into three worlds: the upper world of gods (*swah*); the middle world that we humans

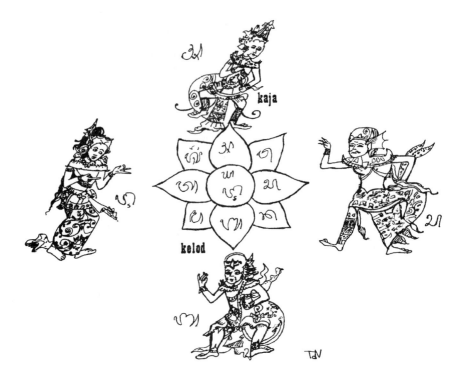

Figure 4   The cosmic map: gods, syllables and colors on a flower petal. The ten syllables written on this lotus petal form an image of the cosmic map. The upper petal points toward the god Wisnu, the syllable ha, and the color black. The petal pointing downward indicates the god Brahma, the syllable ba, and the color red. To the left is the goddess of love, Ratih, who is associated with the nadir, the letter hi, and four colors. To the right (or east) is the god Iswara, the letter sa, and the color white. (The other six gods are not shown).

inhabit (*bwah*), and the lower world beneath the earth (*bhur*). The same tripartite division is applied to the island of Bali, with the mountains as swah, the plains as bwah, and the sea as bhur. Likewise, the head and neck of a person are swah, the torso, bwah, the legs below the knee, bhur. The upstream part of a village, where the temples to the friendly gods are located, is swah; the main village is bwah; and the temple of death and cemetery are bhur. The temples themselves are laid out according to the same scheme, with the offerings to the gods at the "head" (swah) of the temple, and blood sacrifices to demons just outside the gates (bhur). Even the walls around the temples follow the same spatial geometry: at the bottom are images of serpents who coil around the foundation of the world; in the center of the wall there are scenes from the human world; and symbols of the gods and the upper world are placed at the crest or towers of the walls.

All these examples refer to the structure of the "outer world," which at different times may refer to the village, the island of Bali, or the whole cosmos. The Balinese

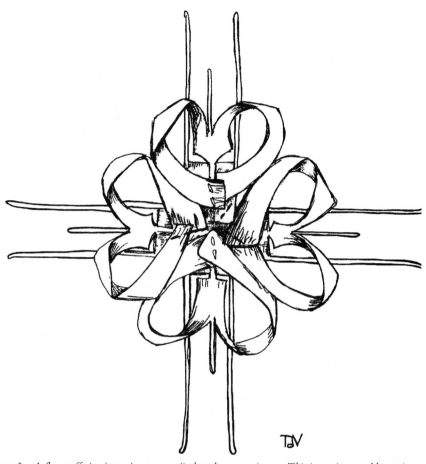

Figure 5   A flower offering (sampian nagasari) *shaped as a cosmic map. This image is created by cutting, folding, and stitching lontar palm blades into an image of a cosmic map. Colored flowers or other symbols are usually placed on it to complete the imagery.*

call all of these the Bhuana Agung, or Great World. But the same map also refers to the Bhuana Alit, or Inner World of the self, the microcosm. In fact, there is supposed to be a direct correspondence between the inner and outer worlds. Ida Bagus chose an interesting example to explain this idea: the relationship between people and their houses.

One day a client came to consult Ida Bagus because he'd felt weak and listless for months, ever since he rebuilt his house. Ida Bagus diagnosed his sickness as *pamali*—a wind in the body that doesn't know where to go, and interferes with one's breathing and other vital functions. According to Ida Bagus, pamali is often caused by having something wrong with the proportions of one's house. For houses belong to the world of living things, and their condition affects the well-being of their inhabitants.

The orientation of the house and its buildings in space is based on the kaja–kelod axis. The main entrance to the house should be a gate in the kelod-kauh corner, while shrines to the gods and ancestors *must* be located in the kaja-kangin corner. The entrance gate is a very important part of the house, because this is where evil influences from the outside can enter. Behind the gate there is often a wall designed to keep out demons. Since minor demons are stupid and only travel in straight lines, the wall can help prevent them from entering.

Inside the walled courtyard that defines the space of the house, there are several types of buildings. Kitchens and rice barns are enclosed on all four sides. The kitchen is located slightly farther seawards than the rice barn, because rice is considered sacred, while eating is regarded as an animalistic act. The main living space is provided by rectangular, roofed pavilions that are usually walled in on only two sides. Here people sit, talk, and work during the daytime. At night they may sleep on a sort of wide platform bed built into these structures, protected from evil spirits by images of guardian figures, and also by the very architecture of the building.

The arrangement of all of these buildings and structures is strictly determined by the tripartite scheme of spatial orientation. The diagram on page 22 shows the cardinal directions: note that kaja is always mountainwards and kelod, always seawards. The spatial alignment built into the structure of the house must be followed by the people within it. For example, one always sleeps with one's head pointed "upstream" (kaja or kaja-kangin). To do otherwise is to risk falling victim to a sickness like pamali. Even the wood used to build the house needs to be oriented as it was when it was part of a living tree. Offerings should be made to each tree, before it is cut down, to explain that it will soon be brought back to life as part of a house. After the house is finished, this promise must be kept. All the parts of the house are symbolically unified and brought to life in a housewarming ritual, which is nearly identical to the ritual used to bring a sacred wooden dance mask to life. According to Ida Bagus, if these rituals are not performed correctly, the house is likely to sigh or moan at night, and the owner may become sick with pamali.

I wanted to know what a person could do, besides having a housewarming, to make sure that their house wouldn't attack them. How does one determine the right proportions for all the buildings? Ida Bagus explained that detailed instructions for this purpose are laid out in architectural manuals called *Asta Kosala*. For example, from the floor of a building to the horizontal beams supporting the roof should be one *depa agung,* the span from tiptoe to the highest one can reach. Other measurements used in the construction of the house are based on other dimensions of the body: the length of one's foot is one *tapak;* the width, one *tapak ngandang;* the span from elbow to fingertip is one *hasta;* the length of the index finger, one *tri adnyana;* the width of one's smallest finger, a *nyari kacing;* and the distance between the two creases in the first joint of one's index finger is called a *tek.* Measurements like these (and others as well) are used to calculate every dimension of the house walls, gates, buildings, the height of the roofs, and the dimensions of the family shrines and temples. The result is a collection of buildings and courtyards scaled to the size of the occupant.

But the physical proportions of the house and its owner are only the first and simplest kind of resemblance between them. Two other aspects of a person's identity also play a role in determining the configuration of his or her house, and the kinds of ornamentation it should contain: wealth and "caste," or inherited rank. There are three levels of cost (expensive, moderate, and inexpensive), and one is free to choose how much money to spend on a new house. But the link between one's rank or occupation and one's house is not a matter of personal choice. The *Asta Kosala Kosali* manuscripts are emphatic on this point. For example:

> . . . it is forbidden to build a greater house than belongs to one's caste. Otherwise one will have a short life, become thin and sick, and quickly die. If one does not die, nonetheless one will be constantly sick. The house of a Wiku, Pedanda or Brahmana may not be occupied by a Sudra or it will be as if they are burnt by a fire day and night.[10]

In other words, to live in a grander house than is appropriate for one's "caste" is dangerous—the energy in the house will be too "hot" to handle. But what does heat have to do with caste? Ida Bagus explained it this way:

> There are regular flows of energy in the human body, some of which are physical (like breathing), and some of which are invisible, like the flow of knowledge gained by reading sacred texts. A teacher bears the responsibility for choosing what his students should read and contemplate. If they choose well, the student will learn steadily, but if they choose badly, and give the student things they aren't ready to understand, the student will not learn and may be harmed, because it is more than they can handle. Too hot! Like a farmer putting fertilizer on his fields—he must not use too much or the plants will be burned. It is the same with a house: an ordinary person trying to live in the house of high-caste people is in danger of being burned by the flow of energy around him—it's more than he can use.

In other words, the spatial orientation of the house is not important in itself but because it channels a flow of invisible energy within the house. According to Ida Bagus, this flow varies according to one's caste identity. But what did that mean?

I already knew a little about the so-called caste system in Bali. Balinese ideas about caste came from India, as part of the Hindu religion that was adopted by many Balinese sometime in the first millenium A.D. In India, where it originated, the caste system divides society into four major endogamous groups or "Varna," which are ranked as follows:

Brahmans: priests and holy men
Ksatriyas: princes and kings
Vaisyas: merchant princes and lesser nobility
Sudras: farmers, craftsmen, and ordinary people

In addition to the four Varnas, Indian Hinduism also recognizes a category of "Untouchables," or people without caste. Caste is linked to occupation: for example, the low status of the untouchables in India is attributed to their "unclean" occupations as butchers, leather-workers, sweepers, etc. Within each of the major Varnas there are many subcastes, traditionally associated with particular occupations. In the idealized Hindu model of caste in India, each caste and subcaste has a predetermined role in society, passed on in families through inheritance and accompanied by specific duties (*dharma*). Caste is inherited through one's parents, and is thought to be based on the balance between good and bad actions in previous lives (*karma*). In the Hindu religion, members of different castes are linked together by mutual interdependence and networks of exchanges. In Bali (as we will see in Chapter 5), early kings made efforts to impose this model of social organization on their subjects as early as the eleventh century A.D. But while some aspects of caste took hold of the Balinese imagination, others (such as the category of "untouchables") were never adopted by the Balinese.

But in 1971, I wasn't especially interested in the history of the caste system; instead I was trying to understand why living in the wrong house could make a Balinese sick. Ida Bagus explained that this had to do with karma, the belief that one's life is predetermined by one's actions in previous lives. Implicit in the idea of karma is the concept of reincarnation. Most Westerners tend automatically to think about this idea in terms of death (the idea that after death, people may be reborn). But from another perspective, what is most interesting about karma is birth: when a new baby arrives, who is he or she (or rather, who was he or she?).

When I asked for some help with these ideas, Ida Bagus suggested that I pay attention to something that seemed to have nothing to do with caste or houses or reincarnation: a calendar called the *tika,* which keeps track of a series of ten different-sized weeks. This seemed like a sidetrack at first, but once I got started, I quickly saw that the tika calendar was directly connected to the "map of the inner world," and the answers to my questions.

THE TIKA: CYCLES OF TIME

The tika is one of two calendars used by the Balinese. The other one is based on the solar year, and closely resembles our calendar of twelve months. But the tika is used for quite different purposes than the ordinary calendar of days, weeks, and months. Physically, a tika is a wooden or painted grid showing 210 days arranged in thirty

THE UKU CALENDAR

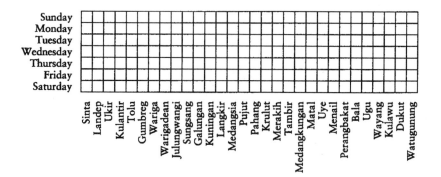

Uku (30 named 7-day weeks)

Figure 6   This diagram shows the 210 days of the uku calendar, depicted as a grid of thirty seven-day weeks. The first day of the calendar is the square at the upper left, the next day is the one below it, and the eighth day is the top square of the second column.

seven-day weeks *(uku)*. Each of the weeks has a different name, and most Balinese can reel off the names of the thirty weeks from memory.

But this is only the first and simplest classification of time portrayed by the tika. In addition to these thirty seven-day weeks, the tika also keeps track of nine other weeks, each of different length. Thus, there is also a three-day week, consisting of three named days: *Pasah, Beteng,* and *Kajeng.* The three-day week is concurrent with the seven-day week, so that if today is Sunday in the seven-day week, it is also Pasah, Beteng, or Kajeng on the three-day week. Symbolic notations (dots, lines, crosses, etc.) are used to superimpose the days of the three-day week on the grid of seven-day weeks displayed on the tika.

In addition to the seven-day week and the three-day week, there are also eight other weeks, varying in duration from one to ten days. The eight-day week or *Astawara,* for example, consists of eight named days. Each of the different weeks has different uses. For example, when a child is born, the parents use the tika to find out what day it is on the Astawara, because the child's Astawara birthday provides a clue to his or her identity in the previous life:

Birthday in eight-day week:	The infant is probably a reincarnation of a:
Sri	woman from the mother's side
Indra	man from the father's side
Guru	brother of the father (uncle), grandfather, etc.
Yama	man from the father's side
Ludra	woman from the mother's side
Brahma	man from the father's side
Kala	person who died as a child
Uma	sister of the mother (aunt), grandmother, etc.

THE THREE-DAY WEEK SUPERIMPOSED ON THE UKU CALENDAR

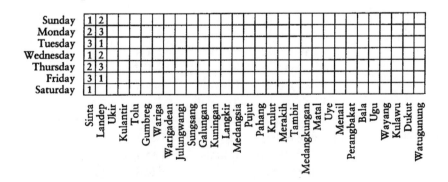

Day 1 = Pasah   Day 2 = Beteng   Day 3 = Kajeng

Figure 7   All ten different weeks, ranging from one to ten days, are included in the uku calendar. Here we see the days of the three-day week superimposed on the calendar. Thus the first day of the seven-day week (square one) is also the first day of the three-day week.

You're probably beginning to see how the tika connects to the concept of reincarnation. But there's more to it than one might suspect, so let's continue to investigate how this calendar is organized. Each cell in the tika marks a date for each of the ten concurrent weeks. For example, there is a one-day week that consists of a single day, *Luang,* so every day is Luang. The two-day week consists of two days, *Menge* and *Pepet:* if today is Menge, tomorrow will be Pepet, and the next day Menge again.[11] The first day of the tika calendar is Day One (Menge) of the two-day week. It is also the first day in the three-day week, the second day in the five-day week, and so forth, as shown in Figure 8.

If all these day names were included in each of the 210 cells, the calendar would have to be very large, and it would also become quite confusing. Instead, small marks on the tika enable a knowledgeable user to identify all ten day names for any given date. This information is important for many purposes. For example, the three-day week is the market week. Instead of holding a permanent market in each village every day, market traders cycle around three different villages, following the day of the market week. This has some obvious advantages for traders (three times the customers!) and for buyers (more selection). The system works well because the market day never changes: some inscriptions, hundreds of years old, refer to markets that are still on schedule today. Imagine trying to keep up with a three-day market cycle using our seven-day week: if the market were held on Sunday, Wednesday, and Saturday this week, it would occur on Tuesday and Friday the following week, making it hard to remember the schedule.

While virtually everyone keeps track of the three-day week, people ordinarily pay little attention to the days of the eight-day week, except when a baby is born. Then, as we just observed, the date on the eight-day cycle is a clue to the child's former identity. But the eight-day week is not the only link between the tika and belief in reincarnation.

THE FIRST DAY IN THE UKU CALENDAR

1-day week:	vacant	day 1
2-day week:	Menge	day 1
3-day week:	Pasah	day 1
4-day week:	Sri	day 2
5-day week:	Kliwon	day 1
6-day week:	Tungleh	day 1
7-day week:	Redite	day 1
8-day week:	Sri	day 1
9-day week:	Dangu	day 1
10-day week:	Sri	day 4
1-day week:	Luang	day 1
2-day week:	Pepet	day 2
3-day week:	Beteng	etc.

Figure 8 A magnified view of the first square shows the date on all ten weeks.

Ida Bagus explained that sometimes children are born while still owing debts to beings in the spirit world. These debts must be paid or the child will be weak and sickly, and may even die. I wanted to know what these debts were, and how they could be paid. Apparently, the parents must visit a ritual specialist like Ida Bagus, who will determine the child's birthday on the five- and seven-day weeks. There are 7×5, or 35 possible combinations, each of which has a particular meaning. Special 35-day calendars provide more information than the tika about each of these days. Depending on where the child's birthday falls on the 5- and 7-day weeks, a particular set of offerings must be made by the parents to pay the infant's debts. The debt-offerings may be placed at the seaside, beside a river, or even in a trough used to feed livestock, depending on the date. Ida Bagus would not tell me what these differences meant. He said that this information could be used for witchcraft if I inadvertently passed it on to the wrong persons. But I could easily see how this ritual could work on the imaginations of the child's parents as it did on mine. Where had this infant come from? what adventures had caused it to fall into debt? and what might happen if the parents didn't pay?

Broadly speaking, the tika calendar links a concept of cyclical patterns to the map of the inner world. At birth, each child is thought to be accompanied by four invisible spirit-children. These spirits are regarded as brothers and sisters of the child, who take up new positions inside the child's body at the four points of the inner compass. When the child emerges from the womb, the four spirit-children are believed to be present in the afterbirth. The afterbirth is placed in a coconut, wrapped with sacred cloth, given offerings, and buried at the entrance to the sleeping quarters: on the right for boys, and on the left for girls. If the family ever leaves the house, the earth where these remains are buried must be dug up to represent all the generations of spirit-children, and taken to be reburied at the new house. Thus as each new child is born, the link between a house and its occupants is strengthened. The four spirit-children are each associated with a direction:

"So when a baby is born it is accompanied by four other spirit-children?" I asked Ida Bagus.

"Yes."

"But even if they're different at birth, don't their identities eventually merge into one? Are my spirit-brothers the same as my sister's? Or my great-grandfather's? Since you call them by the same name, aren't there really only four spirit-children for everyone?"

Ida Bagus had an interesting answer:

"Where is the wind coming from just now?"

"From the sea—from 'seawards' (kelod)," I answered.

"And the wind that blows on us now, is it the same wind that is shaking the trees in the mountains? Is it the same as yesterday's wind? How many winds are there from 'seawards'?"

THE INNER COMPASS AND THE HUMAN LIFE CYCLE[12]

By now I understood why Ida Bagus insisted that I pay attention to the spatial symbolism of the inner compass and the tika calendar. I had grasped the main point he was trying to convey, that all of the offerings and rituals I saw referred to the compass of the inner and outer worlds, and that these offerings were timed by the cyclical patterns of the tika. The next step was to learn to "read" the symbolism of particular rituals. I was particularly interested in following up Mead and Bateson's ideas about Balinese personality. Ida Bagus spent a lot of time helping various high priests (like his elder brother) perform rites of passage for their clients. For example, babies were not allowed to touch the ground until their first 210-day birthday, when a complicated ritual was performed. Why not? What did these rituals mean?

In pursuit of these questions, I began to spend more time observing Ida Bagus assisting with rituals and talking with his clients—the people who came to him for advice, usually about rituals they needed to perform for family members. Quite often he would consult one or another of the sacred texts in his household library, to make sure he was giving the right advice. These texts also included additional information—stories, drawings, and explanations—that helped to clarify the meaning of the rituals. The clients were not particularly interested in hearing about these explanations, but Ida Bagus was fascinated by them and was quite willing to take some time to interpret them for me. Evidently, birth, childhood, marriage, and death were all considered dangerous transitions, requiring the performance of rituals to help the individual pass safely to the next phase of his or her existence. But what were the dangers to be avoided? And what kinds of knowledge or experience were the rituals designed to promote?

Over a period of months, I began to piece together answers to some of these questions. Each ritual had its symbols and meanings, which Ida Bagus helped me to decipher. More intriguingly, I began to see that whole sequence of rituals from birth to death come together in a meaningful pattern. Most anthropological descriptions of the life cycle begin with birth. But when you've read the next section, perhaps you'll agree with me that, in the Balinese case, it makes more sense to begin at the moment of death.

Washing the Corpse

When someone dies in a Balinese village, a drum is beaten to summon representatives from every family in the neighborhood. The drum is made of a hollow log, and it hangs from a tower alongside the neighborhood assembly hall. Every Balinese village includes one or more residential neighborhoods, called *banjar.* When they hear the drum, every family in the banjar is obligated to send one or more family members to help wash the corpse and prepare it for burial. A crowd of people quickly gathers in the house of the family of the dead person. The clothing of the dead person is carefully removed, and the body is washed from head to foot and purified with holy water. The purpose of the holy water, according to Ida Bagus, is to wash away the pollution of death and to prepare the soul of the deceased for the long journey that will free it from earthly ties. For immediately after death, the soul is thought to hover above the body in a state of bewilderment.

Surprisingly (to a Westerner like me), the atmosphere is not solemn; instead there is a bustling crowd of people, talking informally with one another as they go about the business of preparing the body. There are more overt signs of sadness at the death of a child; but at the death of an older person, I had the impression that everyone was more eager to be seen doing their part to help than mourning for the deceased. Death is an occasion when neighbors try to behave like relatives, helping the family of the deceased through a difficult and potentially dangerous time. Banjar members may contribute money, food, or clothing, help to dig the grave, and escort the family with the body to the cemetery. After a final bath of holy water, any wounds on the body are covered with tamarind paste so that they will be healed in the person's next life. Ornaments are placed on the corpse, such as mirrors over the eyes, which are thought to confer clear sight and personal beauty in the next life. A white shroud is prepared,[13] inscribed with an image of the human body labeled to indicate the correspondence of the inner world of the self to the outer world of the cosmos. The parts of the body are marked with letters indicating the *dasabayu* (ten wind-directions), the destination of different aspects of the self at the moment of cremation, when its elements will be dissolved back into the outer world. Additional drawings sometimes depict the passage of the soul at death out of the middle world. Finally, if the family can afford it, the corpse is dressed in new clothes.

These preparations provide a way for neighbors to demonstrate their desire to help the family of the deceased, and in so doing emphasize the solidarity of the community. But the next phase of the death rituals has nearly the opposite effect. For on the appropriate day (ascertained with the aid of the tika), the corpse must be cremated. The cost of cremation varies from expensive to ruinous, and may force a family to go into debt, even to the extent of selling their farm land. All of these expenses are borne by the family of the deceased, not the banjar. The preparation of cremation towers is especially expensive. Various types of cremation towers are appropriate to different castes or sub-castes. Most banjars include members from different castes, and one of the major sources of social friction in the village is the idea that differences in caste represent differences in merit, or one's deserved place in society. The idea of rank, which is implicit in the very idea of a caste system, can often be ignored in people's daily relationships. But the building of a cremation tower[14] and the procession of the family to the burning grounds forces each family to make a very public statement about how they define their position in the social hierarchy.

In the twentieth century, there have been numerous efforts by progressive Balinese to reduce the costs of cremation, and the social tensions they so often exacerbate, either by encouraging whole banjars to carry out their cremations on the same date, and so share the costs of the ritual, or by reducing the amount of time and money spent on these rituals. There is a temptation for ambitious families to carry out cremations with higher-ranking caste symbolism than their neighbors regard as appropriate. The result is said to be that the cremation will not achieve the desired effect of launching the deceased on a successful journey to the next life. Instead, the deceased becomes an angry ghost, unable to take leave of the world, who is likely to take revenge on the family members whose pride caused their predicament. Alternatively, families who lack the necessary financial resources may be tempted to postpone the cremation ritual indefinitely, which can lead to strong feelings of guilt and failure (and fear of revenge from impatient ghosts awaiting cremation).

Ancestorhood

After the cremation tower containing the body has burnt to ashes, a few fragments of bone and ash are gathered and placed inside a coconut wrapped in a yellow cloth, which is ceremoniously carried to the beach, where prayers are offered by a high priest. The contents of the coconut, representing the five elements from which the body was formed, are poured into the ocean where they are thought to dissolve completely into the primal elements of earth, air, water, fire, and ether.

Some time afterwards, another ritual sequence called *nyekah* or *memukur* is carried out by one or more priests on behalf of the family. An effigy of the deceased is created, to which prayers and offerings are made by family members. Then the effigy is burned and the ashes are placed inside a yellow coconut, which is wrapped in a white cloth and carried on a final visit to the shrines of the family temples. Afterwards, the effigy is thrown into the sea, and the soul of the deceased is symbolically released from its earthly existence, to become an ancestral spirit who can be worshipped at the family shrines until he or she is reborn as a human infant. This ceremony is another occasion where proud families have the opportunity to publicly display their claims to high status. If they yield to this temptation, these final rituals of death can be even more costly than the original cremation. In addition to members of the family, many guests (preferably of high social status) may also be invited to witness the nyekah ceremony. While these rites are ostensibly performed for the benefit of the ancestors, they are also a public assertion of status pride that may challenge other families to put on an even grander show.

Birth and Early Childhood

Understanding the symbolism of Balinese death rituals makes it easier to make sense of the rituals connected to childbirth. These rituals portray newborn babies as ancestors who have come to be reborn on earth. Physical imperfections on the child's body, for example, may be interpreted as scars from punishments inflicted in hell for evil deeds in a former life. The birth process itself is considered to be dangerous and makes both mother and child temporarily impure. Indeed, Ida Bagus once suggested to me that birth was the inverse, or complement, to death, which also involves danger and pollution. There are a series of rituals designed to help the child become human again. These rites focus on the inner compass: the four sibling spirits who accompany the child at birth and will help decide the fate of the child as it grows to adulthood.

For the first three months after birth, the child is very vulnerable to witches or sorcerers.[15] If a witch can manage to steal the coconut containing the remains of the afterbirth during this time, it can be used to create a *bebayi,* a ghost that can be sent to attack the witch's enemies. The witch must go in secret to the village's Temple of Death and ask for help from the Goddess of Witches, *Batari Durga.* Then she performs the same ceremonies for the afterbirth that are needed for a human child. The bebayi becomes an invisible servant who can fly into the body of a victim, and will drink the victim's blood until he or she turns yellow and eventually dies. According to Ida Bagus, if the victim goes to a healer (*balian*), the bebayi can sometimes be felt under the person's skin. Only a very powerful healer can persuade the bebayi to leave the victim's body, since it can reappear in different parts of the body until the person's blood has all been consumed.

The bebayi, or vampire spirit, is grown by nurturing the demonic aspect of the four sibling-spirits (*kanda empat*) that every child is born with. Each of these spirits controls 27 *bajang*, a word that can perhaps best be translated as "vices," like anger, jealousy, or thievery. Each bajang has its special place in the inner compass of the child's body. But the birth spirits also have positive aspects, which the ordinary rites of childhood are designed to foster and strengthen. It is thought that children gradually forget their sibling-spirits as they grow older. But when death is near, according to Ida Bagus, our four sibling-spirits appear to summon us and send us on our way to one of the many afterworlds. At that time they are called I Tutur Mengat: "those who remember."

The names of the four sibling-spirits change as the child grows to adulthood. As I'll explain later in this chapter, the same is true of human beings: our identity is thought to change as we move through the stages of the life cycle, and these changes are marked by name changes. But our invisible brothers and sisters always remain with us in some form. In Balinese philosophy, they are the link between the microcosm of the human individual (the Small World, or *bhuana alit*) and the macrocosm (the Great World, or *bhuana agung*). For example, as we just observed, in their negative or demonic aspect, each of the four sibling-spirits controls 27 elemental vices, which are capable of overwhelming us so that we become dominated by one or more of these vices for the rest of our lives. These 4×27 or 108 elemental vices of the human soul correspond to the 108 elemental powers or "demons" (*buta*) of the outer world. In other words, all the demons of the outer world also exist within our bodies, and the rites of childhood are designed to prevent them from gaining control. Within the human microcosm, the four spirit-children in their demonic or elemental state are called the kanda empat buta.

For the first forty-two days after birth, both mother and child are in a state of ritual impurity. The mother cannot enter sacred places like temples, and the child must be protected from witches. At the end of this period, a small ritual called Forty-two Days is performed, in which offerings are made to the child's spirit and the 108 "vices" (bajang), urging them to depart.

The Three-Months' Ritual (*Telun Sasih*)

If the family can afford it, this ritual is performed by a Brahman priest; otherwise it can be carried out by a temple priest (*pemangku*) or ritual specialist (*balian*). The priest dedicates offerings to the Sun God and the Five Great Elements or Demons, (*Panca Mahabuta*). Symbolically, the child is the brother or sister of the four sibling-spirits. Thus the inner world of the child consists of its own spirit and its four sibling-spirits. The same five spirits exist in the outer world of the cosmos as the Five Elements, often represented as earth, air, fire, water, and ether. These dangerous spirits, who rule the demonic forces in the outer world, are asked to witness that their manifestations in the child are given offerings and respect.

The four spirit-children and their accompanying spirits of vices (*bebajayan*) are summoned, so that, along with the child, they can receive offerings and be purified and tamed. The elemental spirits are given particular offerings and asked to use their energies to help the child by making it healthy and strengthening its spirit. As with many Balinese rituals, the aim is to accomplish a transformation, taking elemental powers (buta) that are intrinsically dangerous and bringing them under control.

The focus now shifts to the parents. The priest purifies them with prayers and a sprinkling of holy water, after which they offer prayers to the Sun God, to the Hindu god Brahma the Creator, and to the shrine of their ancestors. Then they pick up their child and carry it in a right-handed circle around a jar of water three times, representing the passage of birth, life, and death.

Meanwhile, two special shrines have been prepared alongside the platform where the offerings are made. One is dedicated to Sang Hyang Kumara, the god of small children, and the other is a hanging cradle containing various offerings and an effigy of a child. The effigy is made from a coconut, which is carved with a human face, wrapped in a cloth, and given toothpick arms and legs to which are attached various pieces of jewelry. In the next phase of the ritual, the child-effigy is washed in the water from the jar, after which the child is also washed. Then the effigy and the child are both carried around the water jar three times by a relative or friend of the mother. The mother touches her baby's forehead with a stone three times, while the effigy is tapped with an egg. The egg and the stone are dipped into the water after each tap. Ida Bagus explained that the stone symbolizes a long life, while the life of the effigy should be as short as an egg.

The mother then exchanges her child for the effigy and is given a bundle of old Chinese coins. While holding the effigy, she says, "The effigy is not mine; my child is a human child" and gives the money to the other woman while reclaiming her child. Various kinds of jewelry (arm and leg rings, and a golden cap for the fontanel) are taken from the effigy and placed on the child, while bits of string are used to replace them on the effigy. When the child is fully washed and dressed, it is made to lie for a few moments in the hanging cradle beside the offerings. The effigy, representing the demonic aspect of the spirit-children,[16] is then given to the priest's helpers, who later destroy it. Meanwhile, the child is given token presents from the family and friends, and then brought to the high priest to be sprinkled with a blessing of various kinds of holy water.

This kind of misdirection—a little theatrical episode that is intended to confuse the demons—is found in many rituals. For example, on its way to the cremation grounds, the tower containing a corpse is carried at a jostling run by bearers who dash off in all directions at each available fork in the path, hoping to confuse any demons who may have been attracted to the corpse. Similarly, as we saw earlier, little walls are often placed just behind a gate, so that stupid demons who try to enter the house or temple hit the wall and are unable to enter. Thus at one level the ritual treats the higher manifestation of the buta (demons/elements) with great respect, while another part of the ritual is designed to take advantage of the stupidity of the elemental vices, like drunkenness or avarice, which can be fooled into following the effigy and accepting the bits of string as replacements for silver chains.

The Child's First Birthday (Oton)

The child's first anniversary (oton) on the 210-day calendar is marked by the most important ritual of childhood. The general structure of the ceremony resembles the three-months' ritual, but several new features are added. The child is given its first haircut and touches the earth with its feet for the first time. The child is also given its "real" name by the priest, who selects the name by divination (for example, by writing several names on pieces of lontar palm leaf and burning them; the one that takes longest to burn or is least damaged is selected). This name may later be changed if the child shows signs of misfortune, such as frequent illness.

In more elaborate versions of this ceremony, a chicken symbolically pecks out the sickness and dirt from the child's mouth. The jar of water reappears, and the child symbolically releases a fish and receives gold rings in return. According to Ida Bagus, this symbolizes a life of small effort and great rewards. Other children are given little cakes, symbolizing the desirable quality of generosity. If the family can afford it, it is customary to hold a *wayang kulit* (shadow puppet performance) to celebrate the birthday. Afterwards, a priest may also perform the *ngaed* ceremony described earlier, in which the parents repay debts the child has carried over from its previous life.

Puberty and Tooth-Filing

There are rituals to mark the sexual maturity of both boys and girls, which are later followed by a tooth-filing ceremony. The most important deity for the puberty ritual is *Sang Hyang Semara–Ratih,* the male and female gods of love. In this ritual they are treated as a single deity of sexuality and physical beauty, who can bestow many favors, including health and good fortune. The child is dressed in the elegant clothes of an adult woman or man in the presence of its extended family. If the family can afford it, a Brahman priest supervises offerings to the ancestors in the household shrine, to the demonic powers (buta), and to Sang Hyang Semara–Ratih. Boys are often given a kris, symbol of male power, while girls may symbolically enact the preparation of rice. Afterwards, all members of the family gather to be blessed with holy water by the priest.

Tooth-filing is performed on six teeth, the incisors and upper canines, which the Balinese regard as resembling the fangs of an animal or a witch. These teeth are filed down just a little, to make them even and remove their resemblance to fangs. The filings are kept in a yellow coconut that is buried in the ground near the household shrine to the ancestors, since they are part of the body the person brought with him or her in this lifetime.

The six teeth are symbolically associated with six vices or "enemies": sadness (*ripu*), anger (*krodha*), greed (*loba*), conceit (*mada*), lust (*kama*), drunkenness (*moha*), and jealousy (*matsarya*). The ritual specialist or priest who performs the tooth-filing is called the *sangging*, a word that also means painter or sculptor. In effect, the sangging is sculpting the human body to remove animal-like traces, in a process of purification that also makes the person more attractive to the opposite sex. The ceremony is accompanied by more offerings to Sang Hyang Semara–Ratih.

Marriage

The marriage ceremony brings us full circle, since it is the last of the life-cycle rituals before death. One of the unusual aspects of Balinese kinship from a comparative perspective is the preference for marriage to a patriparallel cousin (in other words, one's father's brother's son or daughter). This is a form of endogamous marriage (marriage within one's own circle of close kin) that is quite rare.[17] But I can suggest some reasons why this preference might make sense in a Balinese context:

The vast majority of Balinese have traditionally made their living as rice farmers. The rice terraces and irrigation works require nearly constant attention, so farmers seldom leave their villages for long. The usual residence pattern is patrilocal, meaning that sons continue to reside in their father's house compound after marriage, or else build a new house nearby. A common practice is for married sons to add a new courtyard with a sleeping pavilion and a kitchen, while sharing the use of other buildings including the family's ancestral shrines. As time passes, houses turn into mazes of courtyards occupied by cousins who are all descended from the original builder. In this way families can grow into descent groups, called *dadia*.[18] Such a process led to the large cluster of related households surrounding my little bungalow in Sanur.

Large dadia with many members and lots of land are usually the most powerful players in village politics. The preferred form of marriage is within the dadia. My explanation for this preference goes like this: by marrying a cousin from his father's side (patriparallel cousin marriage), a young man ensures that his bride and the resources she controls will remain within the dadia. Such marriages prevent the fragmentation of land or other heritable property and strengthen the descent group. From the bride's perspective, such a marriage means that she does not have to leave her family, and her children will belong to her own descent group. Otherwise, if she marries outside her dadia, she must symbolically cut her ties to her own descent group by

A high-caste woman takes leave of her ancestors in the family shrine at the conclusion of her marriage ceremony. Beside her is her husband, behind them her mother, aunts, and cousins; in front, a Brahmin priest who performs the ceremony.

announcing to the ancestors in her family temple that she is leaving them permanently to join her husband's dadia. Her children will belong to her husband's dadia, and it is believed that she herself will eventually be reborn into his descent group.

One of the most important considerations relating to marriage is the question of what will happen to a family's house (including the land it is built on) and the household ancestor shrines in the next generation. Ordinarily, sons divide the family's farmlands more or less equally (daughters have no customary rights of inheritance). One son (often the youngest) will inherit his father's house and take responsibility for performing the necessary rituals at the ancestral shrine. But if the family has no children, or if the children are all daughters who marry out, then after the death of the parents, the house and its land will revert to the neighborhood (banjar). There will be no one to tend the shrine to the ancestors, and the cycle of reincarnation may be broken. Couples faced with this prospect often decide to adopt a male heir. They usually wait to take this step until their daughters are of marriageable age, in the hope that by then they will have a son. But if all their adult children are female, the couple will try to find a son-in-law who is willing to play the "female" role by cutting his ties to his own ancestral shrine and moving in with his wife's family as their heir. In return for joining their descent group and taking responsibility for their household shrines, he will inherit the couple's house and property as though he were their son. This arrangement is thought to be easier and more "natural" if the son-in-law belongs to the same dadia as his wife and her parents, since they share a common ancestry. To me, these beliefs seemed to follow logically from the importance attached to the idea of reincarnation in the whole cycle of rituals, especially birth and death.

The most common form of marriage is "wife capture," in which the bride is carried off in secrecy by her prospective husband. There are two types of wife capture: mock capture (ngambis), which is very common, and real capture (melegandang), in which the woman may be abducted by force. In neither case are the woman's parents supposed to be aware beforehand that their daughter is about to be kidnapped. In Sanur, village custom allows the bride's father to visit the couple the next morning to ask his daughter if she wishes to go through with the marriage. The father is expected to be suspicious and upset, and must be accompanied by an elder whose job it is to prevent him from becoming violent. If the daughter chooses to proceed with the marriage, the father goes home, and a purification ritual is immediately performed for the bride and groom. Later, the husband's family sends a delegation to make peace with the wife's parents. The successful conclusion of these negotiations will be signaled by offerings and prayers in the wife's household temple, in which she asks forgiveness from her ancestors for leaving them. After the wedding, she will no longer participate in the rituals of ancestor worship in her own family temple. Instead, she will join her husband in performing rituals at his family shrines. The particular sequence of rituals needed to complete the marriage depends on personal characteristics of the bride and groom, including their caste and birth dates on the tika calendar. Marriage rituals also vary slightly from one village to the next. The alternative to wife capture or marriage within the dadia is a form of arranged marriage, which is usually practiced only by aristocrats who wish to avoid the risks associated with wife capture.

Thus, unlike most other Indonesian societies, where marriage is seen as creating a valuable bond or alliance between families, in a Balinese marriage the main theme is danger. For the bride's parents, marriage essentially means the loss of their daughter, unless she marries within her own dadia.[19] The danger of a violent rupture between the families of the husband and wife is reflected in rituals that emphasize the need for purification and avoidance of danger.[20]

Yet despite these dangers, marriage is highly valued. In Balinese society, a married couple is the basic social unit. In fact, it is impossible to belong to the village assembly except as a member of a married pair.[21] It is also possible for a man to have more than one wife, although in general only a small percentage of Balinese households are polygamous. Altogether, I came to see some deep contradictions in Balinese attitudes about the status of women. On the one hand, the complementarity of gender roles is an important theme in many aspects of Balinese culture. But on the other hand, women have traditionally held little power in the Balinese family. Care for the parents is a responsibility of sons, not daughters, and marriage marks the formal end of a woman's relationship to her own family and ancestors, unless she marries a cousin. In the nineteenth century, several foreign observers noted that Balinese women could be sold into slavery by their husbands. Even now, since women seldom inherit property, their economic position in the family is less secure than that of their husbands, brothers, and sons. Divorce is a fairly simple matter, which ordinarily does not involve either priests or government officials. Typically, a wife who decides that she cannot continue to live with her husband will leave him and return to her own dadia, bringing only her personal possessions.

I learned a little about Balinese attitudes towards incest and homosexuality, mostly from my readings. Male homosexuality and transvestism are tolerated in modern Bali, but it is not clear what role homosexuality may have had in traditional Bali, before the arrival of Western homosexual artists in the 1930s. On the other hand, two sexual practices were traditionally subject to strong sanctions: incest, and sexual relations between a high-caste woman and a man of ordinary (Sudra) caste. In the days of the Balinese kings, the latter could be punished by the death of both the man and the woman. In the modern age, this prohibition has become a political issue because of its anti-democratic implications. The prohibition against incest, on the other hand, is still strongly supported. The traditional punishment for incest was to yoke the offending pair together and force them to eat from a trough like animals. The birth of twins of opposite sex is also regarded as a form of incest, which causes the entire village to be regarded as spiritually impure for a period of a month or more. Interestingly, if the babies are born to a high-caste woman, then the birth is not considered impure or incestuous. But in the days of the rajahs, opposite-sex twins born to a commoner woman were taken as slaves by the king. Even today, the birth of opposite-sex twins to a commoner causes the whole village to cancel or postpone major rituals, a rule that does not apply if the mother is of aristocratic caste. This difference in the treatment of twins according to the parent's caste is a continuing source of tension in Balinese politics.

Kinship and Names: Cycles of Personal Identity

The idea that people's identities are not permanent, but rather constantly changing as they move through the stages of the life cycle, is also reinforced by the Balinese language. This is especially true of the terms used for names and kinship relations. The

Balinese kinship terminology is of the type anthropologists call "generational." It is a very simple system that classifies kinship relationships in terms of only two distinctions: gender and generational status with respect to ego (see Figure 9).

The father, father's brothers, and mother's brothers are all called by the same kinship term. The same goes for the mother, her sisters, and the father's sisters. The terminology does not distinguish between maternal and paternal grandparents, and great-grandparents are not even distinguished by gender: they are all known as *kumpi*. The whole emphasis, then, is on generational status with respect to ego. The generation closest to ego is split in two by this principle: one set of kinship terms is used for older siblings and cousins, and another for those who are younger.[22]

This emphasis on generational status is also reflected in Balinese personal names. For example, at birth everyone is given a name based on their birth order: an eldest child is called Wayan; the second child, Nyoman; the third, Made; the fourth, Ketut.[23] But rather than continuing with unique names for the fifth, sixth, or tenth child, these four names simply repeat, so the fifth child is also a Wayan, and the sixth, a Nyoman, and so forth. Like the names of the four-day week, the birth order titles are essentially arbitrary markers in an endless cycle of births.

Generational status continues to be emphasized in later life, through a naming custom that anthropologists call teknonymy. Once someone becomes a parent, their given name changes: they are henceforth known as "Father of (child's name)" or "Mother of (child's name)." Later, as grandparents, their names change again, to "Grandfather of . . . " or "Grandmother of. . . . " Teknonymy (the practice of being named for one's descendants) emphasizes changes in one's social identity as one moves through the phases of family life.

Similar ideas are used to define the relationship between the generations. A major theme in Balinese family life is the heavy burden of inter-generational responsibility.

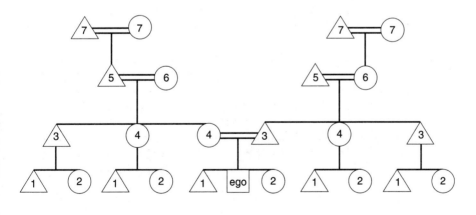

1: Bli (older); adi (younger)   5: kakiang; pekak
2: mbok (older); adi (younger)   6: niang; dadong
3: bapo, aji   7: kumpi
4: meme; weh (if older than mother)

Figure 9   Diagram of kinship terminology

The rituals needed for a safe passage through childhood are performed by parents for their children, a sequence that begins with the rites of childbirth and ends with the marriage ritual. But as soon as the newlyweds have their first child, they must begin to take responsibility not only for their children but also for their elders. Unlike Indian Hindus, the Balinese believe that rebirth can occur very quickly, within a generation or two after the death rites are completed.[24] Perhaps for this reason, Balinese kinship terminology is very "shallow," paying virtually no attention to ancestors more distant than great-grandparents.[25] Indeed, relatives five generations apart call one another by the same kinship term (kumpi) and are classified as belonging to the same generation. This idea has some interesting consequences. For example, when families with young children make offerings at their household shrine to the ancestors, the children are instructed not to pray to their great-grandparents, because they have the same generational rank, and may in fact belong to the same generation. The anthropologist Clifford Geertz has perceptively observed that this folding back of the kinship system on itself results in a kind of "genealogical amnesia," a more or less deliberate forgetting of the identities of one's ancestors.[26] Indeed, the very idea of "ancestors" takes on a different meaning in a society that takes the idea of reincarnation seriously.

Thus, the kinship terminology, the practice of teknonymy, and the use of birth-order names combine to emphasize the generational cycle as the key element in defining a person's social identity. But one aspect of a person's identity does not change with age. That element is their "caste" title, the one part of a Balinese name that is almost never omitted, even in casual conversation. Among members of the three high "castes," who are collectively known as Triwongsa (three peoples), caste titles usually take precedence over the other naming systems, like birth-order names or teknonyms. Because these titles are so seldom omitted, their use marks not only the aristocrats but also the commoners (since the absence of a caste title is equally conspicuous).

The ubiquitous use of caste titles has the effect of constantly reminding people of their relative position in a hierarchy of rank, based solely on birth. As one might expect, in the modern world, few people are entirely comfortable with this system, and it is often at the center of violent political controversies. We'll pick up this story in Chapter 5.

One final point about names is worth mentioning, because it captures the link between personal identity and the flow of time as represented by instruments like the tika calendar. If a person has a long run of illness or bad luck, one of the possible remedies is to change his or her name. To do so it is necessary to consult with a ritual specialist like Ida Bagus, or even a priest, who can go back to the tika and try to make a more exact determination of one's identity, often by tracing birthdays on other weeks. A new name, even if it is kept secret, can help to better synchronize a person with their position in the cycles of time and the compass of space.

THE INNER COMPASS AND THE COMMUNITY

Ida Bagus had assured me that there was a link between the compass of the inner world and the life of the village. At first this seemed like a fairly clear, if somewhat unexciting, idea. The main village temples (Pura Desa and Pura Puseh) are supposed to be located at the upstream (kaja) end of the village; the residential area in the center and the temple associated with the demons or elements (Pura Dalem) are at the downstream (kelod) end, next to the cemetery. These positions fit the spatial symbolism of the inner compass. In Sanur, the actual layout of the village was not so neat, but Ida Bagus showed me other villages where the actual location of the temples and graveyard matched up exactly with this scheme.

I began to realize that there might be more to the idea of a correspondence between the "inner" and "outer" worlds while watching a performance of the famous Barong and Rangda ritual combat. Margaret Mead and Gregory Bateson had been fascinated by this contest. They both referred to it often in their writings about Bali, and also made a film about it, showing dancers going into violent trances. We'll end the chapter with this ritual combat, which gave me the plot for my senior thesis, because it dramatically illustrated a crucial link between the inner compass of the self and the life of the community.

The meaning of the ritual depends on the identity of the two antagonists, Barong and Rangda. Here's how I described them in my thesis:

> The Barong, to the Balinese, is the archfoe of Rangda, the witch who controls black magic and delights in feeding on corpses and the entrails of young children. They are the main characters in a number of religious dramas. These dramas consist of the encounter of the two figures, from which ensues a battle that neither wins. In the course of the drama, the spiritual power (*sakti*) or "soul" (*roh*) of Barong and Rangda may enter their human impersonators, and spectators are often driven into a trance by the mere sight of Rangda.[27]

An actor wearing the mask of Rangda the witch is supported by a helper as he falls into a trance.

The elaborate costumes used by the actors portraying Rangda and Barong are regarded as sacred and are stored inside the village temples. The Rangda costume includes a wooden mask with long fangs, horrible bulging eyes, and a mass of tangled white hair. She also has long, sharp, knife-like fingernails and multicolored, dangling breasts. The Barong, on the other hand, looks fierce but not evil. His costume is a gorgeous baroque creation, which requires two men to operate. His body is covered with shaggy fur the color of burnished bronze, with rows of gilded leather studded with mirrors running along his back and up his tail. The actor in front operates a large wooden mask, snapping the Barong's jaws playfully at invisible butterflies as it strolls down the path of an imaginary jungle.

There are many legends and stories connected with Barong and Rangda, but the central episode in most performances begins when Rangda sends her daughter Rarong to the graveyard to fetch the corpse of a child. Rarong is discovered playing with the dead baby by the Barong, who chases her off. Rarong complains to Rangda, who comes out to do battle with Barong. As they dance into view, Rangda hurls threats at the Barong, who begins to playfully bite and lunge at her. At this point, both actors and spectators may go into trance. Everyone who falls into trance is offered a kris (a short sword with a wavy blade), which they can use to attack the Rangda. Here's what I saw in a performance in 1970:

> One man goes into a violent trance and is held by three men. People jump up all over. A second Rangda appears, and both Rangdas appear to go into trance. The Barong leaves. Several men run up to the Rangdas and attack them with their fists, to which they respond with kicks. In a moment, both are picked up and carried bodily back into the temple. Meanwhile, several men have been given the kris. They run up as if to attack the Rangdas, but stop short and turn their knives against themselves. The explanation that is invariably given for this behavior is that the men with krisses wish to kill the Rangda and are consumed with a passionate hatred, but her power is so great that she turns their knives back on them. Their muscles lock, and they go into convulsions in which their bodies seem to attempt to simultaneously drive the knife home and to tear it away.[28]

Thirty-four years before I saw this performance, the anthropologist Jane Belo observed a similar performance in Sanur, in which the dancers used the same Rangda and Barong costumes I saw. Belo quotes a Balinese who described his feelings while going into trance:

> When Rarong has gone off and the Rangda has come forth, my thoughts grow stronger so that I cannot bear it. In my thoughts I dare to challenge the Rangda and the Pandempat [Rangda's four companions]. When the Barong has done fighting with the Rangda, my thought is to attack Rangda, and my body is very itchy.[29]

Ida Bagus explained that Rangda is the queen of witches and represents all that is frightening in the death temple and the graveyard. But who or what was the Barong?

With the help of Ida Bagus, who wanted to make sure I understood the answer, I asked this question of Pedanda Made (the old priest who had befriended Katharane Mershon). Pedanda Made pulled out a sacred lontar manuscript and selected a passage, which Ida Bagus translated for me. Here's what it said:

Offerings inside the temple to Barong, archfoe of Rangda the witch

A baby in a woman's stomach has four brothers: two from the father and two from the mother. These brothers can make the child sick or well. So the parents must make a small ceremony for the four brothers when the child is born. The four brothers are buried near the house. White rice is put in the east corner, yellow in the west, red in the south and black in the north. Multi-colored rice is placed on the child's bed. The first brother is called Angga Pati, the second Praja Pati, the third Banas Pati, and the fourth Banas Pati Rajah.[30]

When I indicated that I understood the translation, Ida Bagus explained that Banas Pati Rajah, the last of these four "brothers" or spirit-children, is the spirit that animates the Barong. However, the Banas Pati Rajah who enters the Barong is not the birth spirit of a single person, but that of everyone in the village.

"So the whole village fights off witchcraft the way a family does, by guarding and strengthening the birth spirits of the children?" I asked.

"Yes. Banas Pati Rajah, in the Barong, comes from the kanda empat, the invisible spirit-brothers of all the children of the village. The Barong guards the village, just as the kanda empat will guard a family's house, if they remember to perform the rituals correctly. Otherwise, a village is vulnerable, just like a person who has forgotten his or her invisible siblings."

CONCLUSION

I left Sanur in August of 1971 with the feeling that I was just beginning to understand the meaning of what I saw. I was entranced with the idea of the birth spirits of all the children of the village guarding it against witchcraft. And I wanted to understand more about the meaning of performances, like the combat between Barong and Rangda. But it was time to return to college and finish up my senior year.

But what should I leave behind me? Later on in graduate school, I learned that anthropologists usually find a way to pay their informants. But I didn't know anything about this custom then. I hadn't given Ida Bagus any money, but I wanted to leave him something of value. So I gave him my tape recorder, and a few years later he told me what he'd done with it. At first, he used it to record examples of vocal styles in sung poetry (*geguritan*), a difficult art form that he was trying to learn. Playing them on the tape recorder was a good way to practice. But he realized that the machine would eventually wear out and he'd be left with nothing. So he sold it and used the money to build a small traditional pavilion in his courtyard, constructed to be a perfect fit for him according to the principles of the Asta Kosala. He said that sleeping in the new pavilion made him and his family feel safer. Thanks to what I'd learned from him about witches and houses and birth spirits and the cycles of time, I felt that I knew what he meant.

NOTES

9. Jane Belo, *Traditional Balinese Culture*. New York: Columbia University Press, 1970: 87, 93.

10. My translation of a passage from the Balinese lontar manuscript *Swakarma,* blade 36. Lontar manuscript #833 in the library of the Gedong Kirtya, Singaraja, Bali.

11. This is not true for some weeks, in which Menge repeats several times.

12. Balinese rituals are classified as follows: the rites from birth through marriage and preparation for serious study (mawenten) are called manusia yadnya, "rites of persons." The funeral cycle is pitra yadnya, "rites of the dead." The final rite of memukur, which occurs after the funeral and helps transform ancestors into gods is classified as dewa yadnya, "rites of the gods." In addition to these life-cycle rites there are also three classes of rituals:

    a. Dewa yadnya: there are many more rites of the gods.

    b. Buta yadnya: rites of the elemental/chthonic/demonic forces or spirits.

    c. Rsi yadnya: rites of priesthood.

13. The kajang

14. Wadah or bade

15. A witch or sorcerer is someone who secretly studies black magic in order to gain power over others by performing harmful spells or curses. Belief in witchcraft is very widespread in Bali. Faced with a major misfortune like a severe illness, most people will immediately suspect witchcraft and will often consult a religious specialist or minor priest (balian) to discover whether witchcraft is involved and, if so, what can be done about it. The films and book by Linda Connors, Patsy Asch and Timothy Asch (see recommended books and films) portray a trance healer who diagnoses witchcraft in the death of a child.

16. The kanda empat buta

17. Outside Bali, preferential patriparallel-cousin marriage was found among the ancient Greeks and also in some Arab cultures.

18. There are many other names for Balinese descent groups. We'll follow the suggestion of Hildred and Clifford Geertz (1975) and refer to them all as dadia. For a more complete analysis of Balinese kinship and descent, see Geertz & Geertz 1975; Lansing 1983; Korn 1932; Hobart 1979; and Boon 1977, 1990.

19. Even marriage within the dadia is considered dangerous if it is marriage to a first cousin, which is considered "hot."

20. In my opinion, these attitudes towards marriage are partly due to the absence of bridewealth in Bali. The exchange of valuable presents is an important feature of marriage in most other Indonesian cultures, in ceremonies that emphasize the value of the marriage as a permanent alliance between families and/or descent groups.

21. If someone dies, the widow or widower can continue to participate in the village assembly if one of their children of the opposite sex agrees to substitute for the deceased parent.

22. This kinship terminology does not distinguish between types of cousins or the difference between matrilineal or patrilineal relatives, even though (as we have seen) Balinese household shrines emphasize the patrilineal descent group (dadia). But not all Balinese families belong to dadia: the importance of patrilineal descent groups increases for wealthier or more powerful families. I suggest that the current structure of Balinese kinship may be the result of a slow process of change from a bilateral Malayo-Polynesian system (*circa* 4000 B.P.) to a more patrilineal system, linked to the patterns of inheritance created by the invention of irrigated rice cultivation in the late first millenium A.D.

23. There are alternate versions of the first two of these birth-order names: the first born may be Wayan, Putu, or Gedé; the next Made or Nengah.

24. Ida Bagus says that the more sins we have to expiate, the sooner we are reborn.

25. Kinship terms exist for more distant ancestors. Thus *Klab* or *Klabklab* means either great-great-grandparent or great-great-grandchild, etc. But few Balinese are even aware of these terms.

26. There is an exception to this rule: royal families do pay attention to the names and deeds of their ancestors, which are written down in dynastic chronicles.

27. Lansing 1974:75

28. Lansing 1974:79

29. The pandempat are four companions of the Rangda witch, whose identities are somewhat mysterious. They may be linked to the chthonic aspects of the four "spirit-children" in the microcosm.

30. Lansing 1974:81

3 / Art and Everyday Life

"The Balinese may be described as a nation of artists," wrote Geoffrey Gorer in 1936. A year later, having returned from two years' residence in a remote village in the mountains of Bali, Margaret Mead wrote the following description of village life:

> . . . the air was never empty of music, even in the small hours before the dawn, and it was not mere woodland piping but complicated orchestral music that bore witness to many hours of concentrated rehearsal. Upon the hundreds of stone altars of Bali, there lay not merely a fruit and a flower, but hundreds of finely wrought and elaborately conceived offerings made of palm leaf and flowers, twisted, folded, stitched, embroidered, brocaded into myriad traditional forms and fancies . . . Their lives were packed with intricate and formal delights.[31]

Anthropologists who have lived for extended periods in remote peasant villages are generally glad to return to the comforts of university life. This was often the case with Margaret Mead, but not when she returned from Bali. In an essay written soon after her arrival in New York, she asked, "What is the difference between the society in which the arts are an integral part of society, enriching and enhancing it, and the society in which the arts are almost wholly dispensed with?" Like other agrarian societies, the Balinese have to work hard to produce a surplus. But unlike those who simply "eat and drink up" the fruits of their labors,

> . . . the Balinese consume their surplus in far more complicated ways, in rice cakes which the village women have shaped into a goddess; in gold leaf in square yards over cremation towers which will glitter for an hour in the sunshine and then be dismantled and burned; in feeding the members of five orchestras to play at once for one ceremony.

The same theme is echoed in the writings of most students of Balinese culture. "Visitors," according to anthropologist Jane Belo, "were always impressed with the relentless creativity of the Balinese."[32] And in a preface to *Dance and Drama in Bali*, the poet Arthur Waley asked, "What has made Bali a special case?"[33]

The answers offered by Mead and Bateson were based on their psychological portrait of the Balinese, which I found interesting but ultimately unconvincing. I thought it would be worthwhile to find out more about how the Balinese themselves view the arts, before trying out another comparative theory. But my plan soon ran into a potentially serious obstacle: there is no word for "art" in the Balinese language. Was it sensible to investigate the meaning of "art" in a culture that lacks a word for this concept?

Thinking about this problem led me to wonder about the meaning of "art" in Western culture. I came across an essay by a historian, Paul Kristeller, that made an interesting point. Kristeller wrote that "while the various arts are certainly as old as human civilization, the manner in which we are accustomed to group them and to assign them a place in our scheme of life and culture is comparatively recent." The term for what we now call "art" in classical Greece was "techne," but this word also included many other things: "the Greek term for Art (techne) and its Latin equivalent (ars) do not specifically denote the "fine arts" in the modern sense, but were applied to all kinds of human activities which we would call crafts or sciences." This broad definition of art persisted through the Renaissance: "For Thomas Aquinas shoe-making, cooking and juggling, grammar and arithmetic are no less and in no other senses *artes* than painting and sculpture, poetry and music." Kristeller identifies the crystalization of the modern concept of "Fine Arts" and its subsequent popularization with the publication of Diderot's *Encyclopedie* in 1751.[34]

Today, for modern Western art historians and philosophers, "art" usually means the "Fine Arts": literature, music, sculpture, painting, and architecture. All of these kinds of art exist in Bali, along with others, for which *we* lack terms and concepts. So the Balinese certainly create art, even according to the restricted standards of our modern definition. But what concepts of their own do the Balinese use to think about the creations that we call "art"? What role does art play in Balinese lives?

In pursuit of these questions, in December 1974 I moved into a few rooms in the "palace" (*puri*) of the village of Sukawati. The idea of living in a "palace" sounds rather grand, but day-to-day life was quite primitive, even by the standards of my fellow anthropologists. The old palace had been severely damaged by cannon fire in nineteenth-century battles, so it would be more accurate to say that I was camping out in the ruins. Since there was no running water, I either walked to the river or paid villagers to carry water up to pour into basins. There was also no electricity. Cooking was accomplished over a fire or a kerosene stove, and light for reading was provided by kerosene lamps, which also attracted hordes of insects. At night, propping a kerosene lamp on one's mattress under the mosquito net kept out the bugs and made it possible to read, but at the cost of warm smoky air and the threat of fire, made all the more dangerous by the shortage of water.

Still, my "palace" had magnificent gates, nicely overgrown walls, and a bustling village market just outside the south gate. I lived in the compound belonging to the second son of the last rajah, who had been trained in civil engineering by the Dutch during the colonial era. His wife was a woman of "commoner" caste, a nurse who was famous for her courage in the war of independence against the Dutch, when she lived with the guerrillas in the mountains. The engineer and his family lived in the capital city of Denpasar, where he was in charge of roads and public works. Other members of his aristocratic family, numbering about forty in all, continued to live in and around the ruins of the old palace. Quite often the whole extended family would take part in a religious ritual or temple festival in the village. On these occasions the engineer and his family would usually come home for a few days, and we would sit together for hours talking, eating, preparing offerings, and telling stories.

But why live in a "palace," even one as broken-down as Sukawati's? The reason was that everything that I'd read about the arts in Bali suggested that the palaces

Entrance gate to the palace of Sukawati as it looked in 1974

were important centers of artistic activity. Sukawati was famous for artistic innovations during the colonial era (1906–1942), and the neighborhood behind the palace is
still home to some of the most famous storytellers, musicians, and shadow puppet
performers in Bali. By living in what remained of the old palace, I tried to follow the
advice of one of anthropology's founders, Bronislaw Malinowski, who urged his students to pitch their tents right in the midst of whatever was going on.

Setting up house in the palace had one major drawback: it meant that I would
see much less of my old friends in Sanur, twelve miles away. But Sanur was already
undergoing dramatic changes as a result of tourist development, and Ida Bagus
agreed that Sukawati was a better place to learn about the role of art in traditional
Balinese society. Still, I was reluctant to lose touch with him. Soon after my arrival,
his brother came up with a delightful solution to this problem, in the shape of a
broken-down old English motorcycle. A week's work, a coat of paint, and a couple
of Harley-Davidson panniers transformed it into a handsome if somewhat untrust-
worthy machine, with doubtful electrical connections, but a nice loud roar when it
was working. Fortunately, I was seldom in a hurry and didn't really mind if it sometimes took an extra day to get home from a performance in some remote village. But
my most frequent trips on the motorcycle were to visit Ida Bagus in Sanur.

Balinese Brahmins like Ida Bagus are supposed to be teachers, and they like to
make a point with a play on words. The motorcycle provided Ida Bagus with an irre-
sistible metaphor: *Yantra* is an ancient literary term meaning "vehicle," which can be
applied to vehicles like chariots, but also to meditation and poetry as "vehicles" for
the imagination. Ida Bagus pointed out that while my motorcycle would take me

right up to any performance or artist I wanted to see, I would need a different "vehicle" if I wanted to get any further. Otherwise, I'd be like the crowds of tourists who chase after any performances they happen to find out about in the villages, and then stand about staring like oxen, unable to understand a word of what goes on.

The point of the "vehicle" analogy was not lost on me. I knew that Ida Bagus really wanted me to spend less time traveling about and pay more attention to his library of lontar manuscripts. But I was dubious about how much I could learn from these texts. Lontars are written in archaic languages in a difficult script, and I found translating them to be very hard work. Many of them are centuries old, written in an ancient language called Kawi or Old Javanese, which was once the language of the royal courts of Java and Bali but has not been spoken since the sixteenth century. Assuming that I could only manage to get through a tiny fraction of this literature, how would I ever know what was worth reading? Fortunately for me, I did not share these thoughts with Ida Bagus. Instead, I dutifully began to work with him on the first manuscript he selected. It was called *Purwagama,* its subject was the origin of the world, and it was really the beginning of my education in Balinese ideas about art.

According to the *Purwagama,* in ancient times our ancestors lived like animals. One day Brahma, the god of creation, sent his consort Saraswati, goddess of learning, to change our ancestors into human beings. Saraswati created poetry by attaching letters to the inner and outer worlds.[35] This brought human beings into existence by giving them an inner self that contains everything in the whole cosmos. The Goddess continues to be present on the tip of the human tongue, where speech is created. She also lives in written letters inscribed in poems on lontar leaves or, imaginatively, on the petals of flowers like the lotus blossom or the *pudak* (pandanus).[36] On the day of her annual festival, no letters may be crossed out or written words destroyed.

As we saw in the last chapter, these letters form a cosmic map. Without some understanding of this map, which can only be acquired through Saraswati's gift of letters, we remain lost in both worlds. The letter *Sa,* for example, is found in the east in the outer world, and in the heart in the inner world.[37] The words (and the world, and the self) were created with a single sound, represented as the letter *ONG.* Poems, prayers, and serious literature begin with this syllable, called *ongkara.* Properly sounded, it travels through the body, resonating against the sounds of each of the other letters. In this way, it guides the mind or soul through the maze of the body, summoning all the gods and demons (or emotions, qualities, and thoughts)[38] to alertness in their proper places.

Ida Bagus explained that the written symbol for this sound is not the same as the ordinary Balinese letters *o-ng.* Instead, it is a diagram of the cosmos, which can be read as the set of primary elements (air, water, and fire) or the fundamental gods (Iswara, Wisnu, Brahma). The sound is read with a deep, reverberating voice, as the reader tries to push his voice from the bottom of his throat to the bottom of his heart (the center of the body, where the syllable *ONG* is found), and out "into the light" of the reality that lies beyond the inner and outer worlds. According to the *Purwagama,* then, poetry makes us human by creating our inner world, which can contain everything that exists in the outer universe.

The idea of letters as the key to the inner and outer worlds fits into what I had already learned about the concept of the cosmic map. This concept is literally embodied, if you will forgive a small pun, when the bodies of the dead are covered with a burial shroud inscribed with the letters of the cosmic map, placed according to their symbolic positions in the body (with *Sa,* for example, written below the heart).[39] But there was more to this idea than a simple one-to-one magical correspondence between the world and the body. Letters can be used to create poetry, and poetry can become a vehicle for the imagination, allowing it to see beyond the surface appearances of the world. This idea led me to one of the most intriguing Balinese ideas about art, a kind of "beauty" called *alangö.*[40]

ALANGÖ

The concept of *alangö* was first expressed in poems written in a language called *Kawi,* or Old Javanese: the language of the Hinduized kingdoms of Indonesia from the eighth to the fourteenth centuries A.D. Nearly half the vocabulary of Kawi was borrowed from Sanskrit, the sacred language of Hindu philosophy in ancient India. The first Kawi literature was composed by court poets who followed strict rules of metrical construction, based originally on the *wirama* verse form of the ancient Sanskrit epics of India. The Balinese refer to such poetry today as Sekar Agung, the "Greater Blossom," and poets such as Ida Bagus still continue to study and even compose new verses in this genre. Many Kawi poems begin by invoking a deity who is said to exist in the form of "beauty," alangö, in both the inner and outer worlds. Alangö is present in sounds and letters, but also in the beauty of the mountains and the sea. Alangö is a dimension of reality that only becomes available to us through active use of the poetic imagination.

The thirteenth-century poem "Sumanasantaka," for example, begins by invoking alangö as the goddess of beauty, who is concealed in the dust of the pencil sharpened by the poet as he prepares to write.[41] Alangö is said to be "of a finer and subtler nature than the world, which is an object of the senses." It is described as both the ultimate foundation of all that exists and its real essence, a beauty that is imperceptible to the ordinary senses, because it is of a finer texture than the perceptible world, yet pervades everything "from the coarse to the fine" (*aganal alit*). The goddess of alangö is asked to descend into the letters of the poem as if they were her temple.

Obviously, the English words *goddess* and *beauty* are imperfect translations for the concept of *alangö.* After a brave attempt to find a better translation, the author of my Old Javanese dictionary threw up his hands with the remark that translators "must resign themselves to the fact that Old Javanese is exceptionally rich in this area of description, and has developed a variety of means of expressing aesthetic emotion which other languages do not possess." But our inability to express the meaning of *alangö* in a single English word or phrase does not mean that we can't understand the concept, for its meaning is conveyed by the poems themselves. Consider the following passage from the "Sumanasantaka," in which *alangö* is expressed by images of a subtle connection between the soul and the phenomenal world:

> When a woman wishes to die, she asks the gods to return her beauty to the month of Kartika; the loveliness of her hair to the rain-bearing clouds . . . her tears to the dew-drops suspended from the tip of a blade of grass . . .

The same poem describes the waves of the sea as a "flight of crystal stairs down which the poet descends when in old age he ends his life by plunging into alangö." The "forest feels dejected in the month of Asadha," according to another poem, because "its cold makes poets shiver and even sick from the cold." Sculptural friezes along the sides of fourteenth-century temples in East Java show court poets writing poems not only on manuscript leaves, but also sometimes on living leaves or flowers. For us, and I suspect also for the artists who created these sculptures, there is a paradox in stone sculptures intended to last for ages, showing images of poets writing letters on flowers that will not last more than a day. The image points, I think, to the significance of the poetry as a "vehicle" for penetrating the veil of illusion (*Maya*) that conceals the hidden order of the world. The very impermanence of the flowers emphasizes that they, like the letters inscribed on their surfaces, are not an end in themselves, but only a vehicle of alangö.

But was this ancient courtly ideal of beauty still alive in contemporary Bali? Ida Bagus answered this question by pointing out that the *Purwagama* (see page 52) had been completed in 1938 by Pedanda Made, the elderly priest who had been Katharane Mershon's teacher. Admittedly, the *Purwagama* was not a poem, but a religious text. But the old priest had also written several long poems in the Greater Blossom. One of them, the "Kalpa Sanghara" (roughly, "The Final Age of the World" or "The Age of Dissolution") reflected his belief that the fall of the last Balinese kingdoms to the Dutch marked the triumph of brutality at the world's end.

In his youth, Pedanda Made had been invited to teach poetry at three of the major princely courts of Bali: Bangli, Klungkung, and Karangasem. In the 1930s, these courts were able to regain some of their former glories because of a decision by

Ida Pedanda Made Sidemen, perhaps the last court poet of Bali, performs a blessing of holy water in 1974.

the Dutch colonial government to share power with the surviving Balinese princes. This policy enabled the princes to carry out their traditional role of organizing major rituals intended to promote the welfare of their former kingdoms. Reading Kawi literature was an important part of most of these rituals. The young Pedanda Made was recognized as a brilliant teacher of traditional literature, and spent months in each of these palaces teaching Kawi to princes and their courts. In this way, he became perhaps the last of the *kawi rajah* or court poets. For him, the Balinese courts of the 1930s and 1940s were a continuation of the world described in the ancient epics, but a world fast coming to a crude and vulgar end.

Traditionally, while the courts and the homes of high priests provided the usual setting for the study of Kawi literature, the inspiration for poetry was supposed to come not from court life, but from nature. The great poems were composed by wandering poets (*kawi lalana*), who sought alangö in places like the sea and mountains (*pasir wukir*), far from human settlements. This was not a search for solitude, as we might expect, but rather a journey to the source of the powerful emotions from which great stories emerge. The need for such journeys relates to a basic distinction in Balinese thought between "cool" and "hot" places. Cool places are safe and tranquil; hot ones are hot because of the presence of potentially dangerous raw energies. Wild forests, volcanoes, and the sea are generally hot; so are quarrelling villages or families, and angry kings. Peaceful villages are cool, as is a tranquil heart. Local gods and spirits are thought to be everywhere, but "hot" places like wild forests are avoided by ordinary people because they are filled with powerful, dangerous, elemental spirits. "Wandering poets," on the other hand, are urged in well-known passages to seek such places out in their quest for alangö.

TAKSU AND A POET'S RIGHT

Sang Kawi wenang means "a poet's right" to add new verses to his own manuscript (or performance) of even the greatest poetry. Some of the most interesting differences between Balinese and Western ideas about art have to do with the concept of authorship. My teacher Ida Bagus studied Kawi poetry from Pedanda Made, and eventually began to try to compose new verses in the Greater Blossom, to be added to existing poems. Through this practice, new episodes are sometimes added to the old stories. A new episode will typically begin with a quotation from the original text "as said earlier" (*panganyurning kata*), followed by an observation like "the journey is not described, now we speak of what befell the heroes." Ida Bagus gave up a youthful attempt at composing Kawi poetry when he realized that all of the poems he admired had been composed by high priests. Interestingly, he did not feel that the poetry itself was too "sacred." Instead, he found the metrical patterns too difficult, and felt that only someone with the mental discipline of a high priest could master this difficult art. But late in life, after he himself became a high priest in 1990, he returned to the study of Kawi composition.

Not all texts are accessible to everyone. Many sacred texts begin with a firm injunction: "Do not reveal this secret knowledge" (*haywa wera*), or "Forbid to the uninitiated" (*haywa cawuh*). Such texts are often written in such a way that they cannot be understood without the help of oral explanations from a teacher, or else they are filled with obscure allusions, disguising the deeper meaning. Otherwise, weak-minded or untrained students might be tempted to misuse the knowledge contained in the lontars. The study of Balinese literature is regarded as a very serious spiritual undertaking, and manuscripts are treated with reverence as shrines of Saraswati, goddess of knowledge.

Some kinds of literature are more spiritually potent or dangerous than others, and there is a kind of hierarchy of literary languages. Thus Sanskrit is regarded as the language of the gods themselves and is never translated. It is only studied by high priests, for whom it is a language of prayer. Kawi (Old Javanese) is the language of the epics, spoken by the gods and heroes of the previous age of the world. "Literary Balinese," the language of the poetry of the Middle and Lesser Blossoms, is associated with Balinese kingdoms from the present age of the world.[42] It is the language of dynastic chronicles and prose literature.

Poetry in the Greater Blossom is not translated into modern Balinese, which would entail the loss of its metrical structure. Instead, Kawi poems are read or recited in the original, a stanza at a time, by a reader called the *juru baca* ("master of reading") who takes care to follow the shifting melodic patterns of particular poems. After each stanza is sounded, a second person known as the *juru bebasan* ("master of language") translates it into modern Balinese. From time to time, other listeners may interrupt to correct or comment on the rendition of either the original text or the translation. These readings are usually held in conjunction with major rituals such as temple festivals, and allow everyone within earshot to enjoy (and gradually learn) the ancient stories. There are also occasional competitions to judge the best juru baca and juru bebasan.

The "master of language's" task includes interpretation as well as translation. Witty comments on obscure meanings, double-entendre, or metaphors are particularly appreciated by those within earshot of a poetry reading. For this reason, master of language is an honored role, akin to that of a teacher or priest. In dramatic performances, this function is taken over by actors called *penasar,* a word that means not "translator" but "one who is the foundation." A translator is the "foundation" of any performance because he has the power to control the information that is conveyed to the audience by the "sounding of the text." Many kinds of dramatic performances are based on episodes from poems of the Greater, Middle, or Lesser Blossoms, and use long quotations from their written sources. Performers often came to visit Pedanda Made (and after his death, Ida Bagus) to study the poems, memorize the metrical patterns of selected verses, and create artful translations that could be used in their performances. For example, a well-known *Arja* dancer, who broadcasts weekly programs on the radio, made regular visits to study at the priest's home, sometimes creating new verses in the Lesser Blossom with the help of Ida Bagus. This kind of composition is also sang kawi wenang (a poet's right).

As someone looking at this literary tradition from the "outside," I was puzzled by the question of authorship. If poetry and stories are constantly being reworked (and the same is true of other artistic genres, like music and painting), who then is the "author"? Poems often are not signed, and even if they are, the authorship of new "episodes" is unclear. Similarly, new pieces of music created by one village orches-

THREE GENRES OF BALINESE LITERATURE

Greater Blossom Poetry (kekawin):

Old Javanese language
Wirama meter: each stanza contains four phrases of identical length.

Middle Blossom Poetry (kidung):

"Literary Balinese" language
Varying numbers of phrases (usually four) with varying numbers of syllables, ending with a
    regular pattern of vowel sounds
Usually sung without translation, and formerly accompanied by musical instruments

Lesser Blossom Poetry and Literature (geguritan, pupuh):

"Literary Balinese" language
Each stanza contains the same number of phrases, but the component phrases can vary in
    length. Each phrase ends with a specified vowel sound.

tra may soon be heard in dozens of other villages, with hardly anyone aware of the identity of the composers. In the visual arts, beautiful images are constantly copied, with no indication of the identity of their creator. There is a constant, ongoing process of borrowing, which to us might appear to be nothing less than rampant plagiarism. Why don't the "authors" care?

This question is not easily answered, but I believe that part of the answer has to do with a unique Balinese concept, the *"taksu."* The commonplace meaning of *taksu* is a household shrine where one's family ancestors are invited to alight on special holidays, to receive prayers and offerings from their descendants. But recall that according to the Balinese concept of time, after the final rites of purification have been performed, the ancestors are free to be reborn as children into their own families. Most villages have "taksu healers" (*balian ketakson*), who can go into trance to contact ancestral spirits through the taksu shrines, to diagnose the causes of illness or affliction that may be visited on the living by angry ancestors or witchcraft. But *taksu* also has another meaning: great performances, and great performers, are said to "have taksu." As soon as someone begins to learn a particular art form, they make offerings and ask for help at their taksu shrine. Such offerings are continued for as long as the performer continues to practice his or her art. Actors, singers, and musicians are encouraged to lose themselves in their performances by giving themselves up to their taksu, and lackluster performances in which the actors never succeed in "becoming" their characters are said to lack taksu.

TAKSU AND THE PUPPETEER PEOPLE

I learned more about the importance of *taksu* from some of my most interesting neighbors in Sukawati: a famous "clan" or extended family of shadow puppet (*wayang*) performers called the "Puppeteer People" (*soroh dalang*). Balinese villages are laid out along dirt paths with tall earthen walls on either side. At intervals in the walls there are carved wooden gates leading into the courtyard of each house.

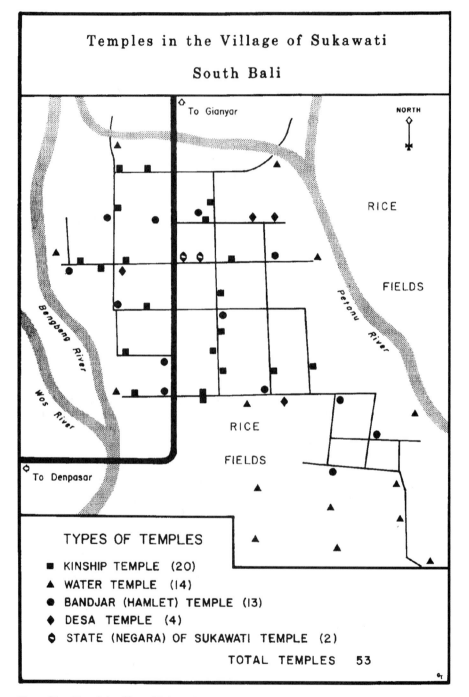

Figure 10   Map of the village of Sukawati

Behind the east wall of the palace in Sukawati, there was such a row of houses, half a dozen of which were home to members of the "Puppeteer People." These families were all related, and for generations they have been among the most famous and successful shadow puppet performers in south Bali. Several times a week, one or more troupes of the Puppeteer People would pack up their instruments in a pickup truck and drive off to perform for a temple festival or rite of passage in a nearby village.

Several different kinds of artists are needed to put on shadow puppet performances. First and foremost is the *dalang* or puppeteer himself, who must be able to quote long passages in Kawi from memory, and spontaneously translate them into Balinese using different voices for each puppet, meanwhile also controlling the orchestra by tapping on the puppet-box with a wooden knocker held in his foot. Different patterns of knocks cue the orchestra to play different melodies. The puppeteer has two assistants who hand him the puppets, and is accompanied by four or more musicians who play the most technically demanding style of Balinese gamelan music. The puppets are themselves works of art, carved from buffalo hide into flat images of gods or heroes, with beautiful painted filigree patterns that throw exquisite patterns of shadows when held up to the light of an oil lamp.

Among the Puppeteer People, all of these jobs are usually performed by members of the extended family. Each new generation of children is exposed to the music rehearsals and performances from the time they are infants. But which of the children will get the taksu? Which child will show an easy mastery of music or languages, form, or color? Which one can invent endless new adventures for the heroes of the ancient epics that will attract a steady supply of customers eager to hire the Puppeteer People to perform? And which children will become farmers and work the family's lands, since they failed to receive the taksu? Such questions indicate that taksu has a special meaning in the context of the arts: we would call it a kind of talent or charismatic gift, which can be passed on from generation to generation through the taksu shrine. This idea makes the question of the "authorship" of performances or texts somewhat ambiguous. I often heard it said that to perform well it is necessary to give up one's self to the performance. Those for whom this is difficult probably lack the taksu for this kind of creativity. For us, artistic creations are often regarded as expressions of our "deepest" selves, and their permanence is connected to our ideas about immortality. In Bali, it seems that immortality belongs to the taksu, and one's individual "self" at any given moment is not regarded as an "author" who spontaneously creates something completely new. To further complicate the picture, the verbal form of the word *taksu* is one of the terms used to describe going into trance possession. "Trance healers" (*balian ketakson*) may be "entered" by a taksu, but this process can also be described as the healer giving over control of her body to one of the "gods" or spirits that lives inside her and forms part of her being. As we have seen, the inner world of the self is not seen as a single unity, but a whole universe. To us, there is quite a difference between the idea of the taksu as a gift from ancestral spirits or as a latent part of one's own personality or "inner world," but in Balinese thought these are two equivalent ways to describe the taksu. In fact, the shadow puppet performances themselves play upon this very contrast between the inner and outer worlds.

These performances are the most "literary" and sophisticated of the Balinese performing arts. There is a special kind of Kawi poetry, called Kawi Dalang, which consists of episodes quoted from the ancient epics mixed with scenes and verses that have been added or embellished over the years in performances. Puppeteers pay close attention to the complex metrical patterns of written Kawi, but they add vocal ornamentation to make the stories more attractive. The passages quoted from Kawi epics must be accurate, or knowledgeable people in the audience will question the puppeter's ability. But they also need to be well integrated into the story, lest the audience become bored and leave. Good performances are supposed to be "illuminating": puppeteers try to choose stories that fit the occasion and help the audience see into their own inner selves. Shifting the audience's attention between the inner and outer worlds is considered necessary to accomplish this goal. For example, consider this passage about shadow puppets from one of the best-known works of classical literature, a story of the hero Arjuna (*Arjuna wijaya*):

> Blinded by the passions and the world of the senses, one fails to acquire knowledge of oneself. For it is as with the spectators of a shadow puppet performance: they are carried away, cry and are sad because what befalls their beloved hero or heroine. . . . and this even though they know that it is merely carved leather that moves and speaks. That is the image of one whose desires are bound to the objects of the senses, and who refuses to understand that all appearances are only an illusion and a display of sorcery without any reality.[43]

A wayang *(shadow puppet) performance. At the center, the* kayon *(cosmic mountain/tree of life), flanked by the four clown/translators.*

The staging of shadow puppet performances is deliberately structured to raise questions in the minds of the audience about the interplay of perception and reality. The puppeteer is seated behind a cloth screen, which is illuminated by the flickering light of an oil lamp. Dozens of carved leather puppets are used to represent the characters of ancient tales drawn from the epic stories of the Mahabharata, Ramayana, and Prince Panji. The puppets are richly painted, but appear on the audience-side of the screen only as flickering shadows, suggesting that the world of the gods and heroes (on the opposite side of the screen, where the puppeteer sits) is so brilliant that it is beyond human sight or imagination. The screen represents *maya* (illusion), which separates us from the "real" world of the gods. But in another sense, all of the gods represented by the puppets also exist inside each of us, in the inner world of the self. Each performance begins with the puppeteer summoning these gods from their places in his inner world and also from the outer world, using the letters and sounds of the cosmic map. The puppeteer constructs a world of pure illusion, mere dancing shadows, which is paradoxically also the "real" world of the gods and his own inner reality. Each audience—the divine puppets and the human spectators—appears as a play of shadows to the other. The puppeteer animates the puppets, but, in another sense, they animate him, since they represent the powers that create both the inner and outer worlds.

The Balinese word for the shadow puppet is *wayang,* related to the word for shadow or reflection, *bayang.* As one puppeteer explained, "*Wayang* means shadow, reflection. Wayang is used to reflect the gods to the people, and the people to themselves." Because wayang creates a world of illusion that is paradoxically more real than the perceptible world, it is an especially suitable vehicle for alangö. The puppeteer calls forth *sastra ning sarira,* the "written language inside the body," and uses it to create a world of illusions that is both "manifest" (*sakala*) and "unmanifest" or "immaterial" (*niskala*). Watching a wayang performance late at night in a Balinese village, with no illumination except the oil lamp casting the shadows of the puppets, one sees that the boundaries between the inner and outer realities—imagined worlds, the world before our eyes, and the worlds of past and present that we take to be "real"—are forever shifting and in flux.

ART IN THE VILLAGES

The concepts of *taksu* and *alangö* help explain why art is taken so seriously in Bali. But what does art have to do with the lives of Balinese who are not professional performers, poets, or priests? To answer this question, we need to become better acquainted with daily life in a typical Balinese village like Sukawati. We'll start with the local residential neighborhood, the *banjar.*

Earlier I described the banjar as a residential neighborhood made up of streets flanked by rows of houses, hidden behind continuous earthen walls. This makes it sound rather empty, but actually nothing could be further from the truth. From sunrise to sunset the streets are lively places, with people hurrying off to the fields or the market, carrying grass to feed their livestock, or on a hundred other errands. Most banjars have several small shops where people can buy household items, eat a snack, or chat with their neighbors. At major crossroads there is usually a small temple and a large

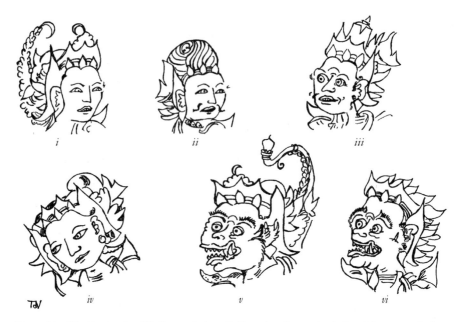

Figure 11   The iconography of Balinese paintings. Balinese drawings and paintings follow a standard iconography that instantly defines the character of animals, gods, or humans. Human heads are usually shown in three-quarter view; animals in profile. The headdress or hairstyle indicates social status. Several examples are shown above:

*   i) Refined aristocratic male (note the small teeth, narrow nose and thin lips, absence of facial hair, and simple fine-line eyebrows). His headdress shows him to be a heroic Ksatriya warrior or prince.*

*   ii) Priest or holy man (identical to the prince except for his priestly headdress, called* ketu).

*   iii) Coarse but not demonic king (note the bulging eyes, joined eyebrows, facial hair, and crown).*

*   iv) Queen (her refined facial features show her noble character, and her crown shows that she is a ruler).*

*   v) Monkey prince (his animalistic character is shown by his bulging eyes, facial hair, and fangs, while his princely status is indicated by his headdress (identical to* i).

*   vi) Demon (raksasa): the round, bulbous eyes, facial hair, joined eyebrows, and fangs indicate that he is a demonic character, while his simple headdress shows his low status.*

roofed pavilion belonging to the banjar. Each banjar controls the land around it, as we've already noted, and can reallocate houseyards to newcomers if a house becomes vacant (as when a childless couple dies). Everyone living inside a banjar is obliged to attend monthly meetings at the banjar pavilion and must pay a fine if they fail to arrive on time. As we saw in the last chapter, banjar members have important ceremonial duties: when someone in their banjar dies, every family must send a representative to help the bereaved family. Banjars also maintain their collective property, such as the streets or paths between the houses; ditches for running water from the irrigation canals, which are routed through banjars wherever possible to provide running water; and public buildings like the assembly pavilion. In colonial times people were often mobilized by banjars for forced-labor projects like road construction.

Each banjar has its own temple, where offerings are made to the local gods to promote the welfare of banjar families. Many banjars own a gamelan orchestra, whose main function is to play at these temple festivals, but may also perform on other occasions. I used to like to walk through Sukawati in the late afternoons past the banjar pavilions, to listen to the sound of children practicing music on their banjar's gamelan instruments. Rehearsals by their fathers usually began a little later, after they had had time for a bath and some dinner.

Sukawati is a fairly typical village with thirteen banjars, mostly inhabited by people anthropologists would classify as "peasant farmers." Two banjars are home to large extended families of artists: the banjar of the Puppeteer People, and Banjar Sangging, many of whose members belong to the Carver People (*soroh sangging*). The carvers practice their art on both wood and stone, creating reliefs used to decorate houses, temples, and other buildings, as well as free-standing sculptures used as decorations in these structures (or to sell to tourists). Most of them are also skilled at painting and drawing. They possess a rich, centuries-old tradition of sculptural and architectural ornamentation, with detailed rules about the kinds of designs and images that are appropriate for particular uses. While the Carver People are often hired by outsiders to decorate new constructions, their work is also to be found everywhere in the Sukawati. Most houses have at least some carved panels and architectural ornaments, and one of the most popular ways to spend extra income is to refurbish one's home with new pavilions, ancestral shrines, or a fancy entrance-gate. The iconography is so well-defined that it is common for several carvers to work at the same time on the same project, their designs meeting somewhere in the middle.

The banjar of the Puppeteer People also includes a family of superb goldsmiths, and elsewhere in the village there are many musicians, poets, dancers, and other performers. All of these artists live side by side with farmers, laborers, and traders, who make up the vast majority of village residents. Yet the dividing line between these occupations (artist, farmer, trader, or laborer) is not very firm. Many farmers are skilled musicians or dancers, and some are fluent readers of poetry in the ancient languages. As the taksu is passed along in families from generation to generation, the knowledge and skill required for very technically demanding arts such as shadow puppetry or goldsmithing remain part of a continuous tradition. Depending on their virtuosity and the market for their skills, some families may be able to support themselves primarily by their art for years. But when this is not possible, artists fall back on typical peasant occupations like farming.

I was curious about how this integration of art into village life had developed. It seemed possible that it was quite recent: perhaps in the days before the Dutch conquest of Bali, the artists had been primarily supported by the courts of the nobility, and had only become part of village life in the past century. In pursuit of this question, I found my way to the little office of the Government Archaeological Service, where a Dutch-trained scholar named Dr. Sukarto Atmodjo was working on translations of royal Balinese inscriptions. There are about 270 such inscriptions, written on stone and copperplate, which began to appear in Bali in the ninth century A.D. Most of the inscriptions were letters or proclamations from a Balinese king to the inhabitants of specific villages, providing detailed rules and instructions regarding village boundaries, taxes, and the penalties for various offenses. I learned that many inscriptions also provide considerable information about the role of art and artists in the village. For example, the earliest known inscription, Sukhawana A1 (issued in A.D. 881),

Sculpture of a demonic guardian to an entrance gate, created by a Balinese sangging sculptor

established a "refuge for people traveling over the mountains" in a mountain village beside the road leading between north and south Bali. The inscription contains a list of various types of artists encouraged by the king to live in the village, who would be exempted from paying taxes to the king as long as they did so. Fourteen years later, another inscription urged artists and performers to take refuge in the village of Bebetin:

> . . . if there should take refuge and live there goldsmiths, blacksmiths, coppersmiths, *pamukul* musicians, singers, *pabunjing* musicians, drummers, flutists, *topeng* dancers, or *wayang* (shadow puppet) performers, then their *tikasan* (tax) must be given to the Fire Temple.[44]

In many of these thousand-year-old inscriptions, mention is made of traveling royal performers (*agending i-haji*) who are empowered to support themselves by collecting taxes in the king's name for their performances in the villages. In other inscriptions, performing art groups based in villages are taxed at a low rate, the amount varying, depending on whether the group sings, dances, performs theatrical plays, or plays instrumental music. Altogether, the royal inscriptions showed that from the earliest moments in the history of Balinese kingdoms, the arts were not based exclusively in either courts or villages, but flourished along an axis between them. Designated "royal performers" regularly visited the villages, while accomplished village artists would be rewarded for performing at court.

But why were the kings so interested in the arts? For that matter, why was art so important in modern-day villages? The best way I could think of to approach this question was to pay close attention to the kinds of events in the village that involved the arts. Who paid the artists, and for what purposes? This question was easily answered. The main source of patronage for most artists turned out to be village temple festivals. In Sukawati, for example, there are a total of fifty-three temples, each of which has at least one festival per year. These festivals require music, offerings, prayers, and poetry readings, and if the congregation can afford it, various types of dramatic performances (many of which are mentioned in the ancient inscriptions). I found the same pattern in Sukawati's neighboring villages: most had dozens of temples, each of which celebrates annual festivals that provide a continuing source of patronage for local artists.

Some important temples even have their own endowments, generally a block of rice terraces. Members of the temple congregation share the labor of working the temple's fields, and after the harvest is sold, the net proceeds are used to help pay for the festivals. These temple lands are not taxed, and the royal inscriptions indicate that this kind of endowment was often created by early Balinese kings. Today, every banjar in Sukawati has a temple, and members of all thirteen banjars unite to carry out the festivals at the three village temples. In the evenings, I often joined my neighbors on visits to nearby temple festivals to watch the performances. With so many temples in the area, each on its own calendrical schedule, it seemed that there were few nights when I could not find a festival or a rehearsal within walking distance from the palace.

But while the link between temples and the arts seemed obvious once it occured to me, I also needed to be able to provide some proof of its existence in my dissertation.

So I did a quick survey and found a strong statistical correlation between the number of temples in a region and the number of orchestras and performing art groups. The same broad pattern also held for other arts, such as stone and wood carving, painting, and literary groups: the more temples, the more artists.[45]

ART, RITUAL, AND TEMPLES

While the question of how the arts are supported in the villages had a fairly simple answer, the answer itself generated new questions. Why was art so important for temple festivals? And why were there so many temples? Why would ordinary families with an average annual income of less than five hundred dollars devote so much of their time and resources to temple festivals?

Most families belong to half a dozen or more temples: one for the banjar, two or three for the village, one or more for their descent group, and several more "water temples" if they are farmers. A typical family devotes several weeks of labor (and considerable expense) each year to "carrying the temples on their heads" (*ngayah pura*). For the most part, these expenses do not go for things like salaries to temple priests but for temple festivals or the ornamentation of the temple itself. The more I looked into this question, the more I was struck by the fact that Balinese temples are almost entirely given over to the arts. Physically, the temples are covered with sculptural friezes and ornaments based on an elaborate religious iconography. Inside, during the festivals, there are no sermons, pledges of faith, or exhortations by the priests. The major sacrament is a simple blessing of holy water coupled with a few short prayers. But this sacrament, which lasts only a few minutes, is embedded within a kind of festival of the arts that often goes on for three days. Temple festivals often include music, dramatic performances, poetry readings, shadow puppets, and an ever-changing display of beautiful offerings to the gods, made of flowers, fruit, and colored rice cakes.

While the religion of Bali is nominally Hindu-Buddhist, this pattern of worship is quite unlike the Hindu and Buddhist rituals practiced elsewhere in Asia. A typical Hindu temple in India or Nepal is an enclosed building with shrines to a god, tended by priests. The temple is never left empty: any Hindu may visit it at almost any time, usually bringing some offerings and asking for the god's blessing.

Balinese temples differ from this pattern in nearly every respect. Physically, they are not closed buildings, but rectangular courtyards open to the sky, with a row of shrines and altars to several gods located at the "upstream" or "mountainwards" (*kaja*) corner of the innermost courtyard. The gods are not thought to be present in the temple at all except on the dates of the temple's festivals, and consequently the temples are usually left empty. But on festival days the entire local congregation is expected to appear and help entertain the visiting deities. Only those who belong to a temple's congregation ever visit it, not because others would be prevented from entering (even tourists are freely admitted) but because each temple is really a sacred space where a specific congregation (a banjar, a descent group, etc.) pays homage to its gods.

Why are Balinese temples so unlike other Hindu or Buddhist sanctuaries? Part of the answer has to do with the origins of Balinese religion. As we saw in the introduction, the Balinese share a common ancestry with the Malayo-Polynesian peoples who settled the islands of the Pacific several thousand years ago. Archaeological research has shown that the early Polynesians worshipped a pantheon of nature gods and ancestral spirits in temples called *marae:* open rectangular-walled spaces, with a row of upright stones or shrines at one end where the gods were invited to alight during ceremonies of worship. The major religious rites in Polynesian societies were festivals in which local congregations offered the fruits of their gardens, forests, and fish nets to gods who personified the forces of nature. All this is very close to the Balinese pattern and strongly suggests that Balinese temples owe as much to their Malayo-Polynesian heritage as they do to the Hindu and Buddhist religions.

But the main focus of attention in Balinese temple festivals is not the row of shrines to the gods in the inner sanctum. Most Balinese temples contain an inner courtyard, an in-between space dividing the realm of the gods in the inner courtyard from the outside world.[46] Widening this border or division into a space where an orchestra can be placed and actors or puppeteers can perform creates a zone where the world of everyday life overlaps with the world of the gods in the inner sanctum. In temple festivals, this middle courtyard becomes a performance space where actors and actresses portraying mythic episodes from the lives of the gods and heroes may go into trance, possessed by the spirits of the characters they portray. Performances in the middle courtyard are addressed to both audiences at once: the gods for whom the festival is being held and the human audience. Here, the boundaries between the three worlds (*triloka*) can sometimes shift. What happens in this space gave me the key to my dissertation.

At first, it didn't seem that the arrangement of the enclosed courtyards in the temples was particularly meaningful. The innermost courtyard of each temple, where the shrines to the gods are located, is called the *jeroan,* the inner sanctum. Here offerings are dedicated, and groups of worshippers are summoned by the priests to kneel on the ground, light a stick of incense to carry their prayers aloft, and raise a flower petal above their heads for each of the major gods invited to the festival. The priests call out short prayers in Balinese as the congregation raises their flower petals in unison. High priests may be hired to add Sanskrit prayers and offerings to those of the congregation. Afterwards, the priests circulate through the crowd of seated worshippers, sprinkling them with holy water and encouraging them to sip a few drops. Finally, a blessing of a few grains of consecrated rice may be handed to each person, who eats a few grains and sticks the rest to their Cakra points on the forehead and at the base of the neck (the Cakra points are yet another version of the cosmic map applied to the human body). Holy water is also sprinkled on the offerings brought by married women for their families, which are arrayed in front of the shrines to the gods. The gods are thought to take the invisible essence of each offering when the prayers are offered. Afterwards, the offerings are taken home and given away as "leftovers" to friends and neighbors, though never to someone from a higher caste. As a person without caste, with an ever-widening circle of acquaintances, I learned to look forward to the day after temple festivals when I would receive basket after basket of fruits, cookies, and rice cakes.

But the prayers and offerings to the gods actually comprise only a small part of a typical temple festival. There is a special genre of artistic performances, called

A wali *dancer*

wali, which are held for the benefit of the gods in the inner sanctum. An example of this type of performance is *wayang lemah,* a kind of shadow play that is meant to be appreciated only by the divine audience. Since human beings are not part of the audience for *wayang lemah,* there is no screen, only a string to rest the puppets against. The gods have no need for a screen since, unlike humans, they perceive reality directly. Since there is no need for shadows, the performance can be held in the daytime. And since the gods understand Kawi perfectly, there is no need for translations, and the entire performance occurs in Kawi, without any translations into Balinese.

   In sharp contrast to the wali performances for the gods, there are also performances called *balih-balihan,* "things to watch," which are held just outside the temple gates or in the outer courtyard. These performances are addressed exclusively to the human audience, and do not concern the gods. People who do not belong to the temple congregation are free to come and watch these performances, in which the only language spoken is usually ordinary Balinese.

Between the inner sanctum and the temple gates[47] or outer courtyards is the middle courtyard, where a wide variety of performances called *bebalih* are held. These performances are addressed simultaneously to both the human audience and the gods of the inner sanctum. Here the reading groups sit to read and translate the poetry of the Greater Blossom; here actors portray stories from the ancient epics and court chronicles; here orchestras play, shadow puppeteers set up their screens, and actors or dancers may fall into trance, their bodies temporarily occupied by the characters they portray.

When a bebalih performance begins, usually well after the sun has gone down, the actors begin to re-enact a story drawn from historical or mythical past. At first, they are actors, re-enacting "real" events from the past. The appropriate languages (such as Kawi) are used by the heroic characters, with translations into Balinese by their clownlike servants or penasars. Meanwhile, the spirits of the real gods and heroes whose exploits form the basis of the stories have been invited into the inner sanctum, and it is assumed that they may be watching the performance. The separation between the audience and the actors, worshippers and gods, past and present, imagination and reality, and the inner and outer worlds can sometimes, startlingly, appear to vanish. I remember one evening when a bebalih performance had something of this effect on me.

A CALON ARANG PERFORMANCE AT THE TEMPLE OF DEATH

The village temple devoted to the frightening gods and goddesses associated with death is called the Pura Dalem. It stands on a grassy knoll by itself, beside a huge old banyan tree and a graveyard. At one time it must have marked the seawards border of the village, but nowadays there is a whole block of banjars a little past the graveyard, closer to the sea than the temple. Balinese who say they want to become healers or test their personal fortitude sometimes come here to spend the night in meditation. However, someone who secretly wishes to learn black magic is instructed to do the same thing: spend the night at the Pura Dalem and ask for the help of the Queen of Witches, Rangda (or Durga). People told me that only strong-minded individuals could spend the night in this temple. Quite frankly, it all sounded a little like something out of a boy's adventure story: a challenge to spend the night in the Haunted House and face the evil witch. But as I learned more about the temple, I began to lose my skepticism. The association of the temple with death is perfectly real: the graveyard is in constant use, as bodies are buried and eventually dug up for cremations. It was also the place where a dozen villagers accused of being communist agitators were taken to be murdered during a period of anti-communist hysteria in 1965. I was told that they had been killed with knives (the short Balinese sword, or kris), and their blood had flowed outside the temple gates like that of the animals sacrificed there at every temple festival. The same theme of human sacrifice came up in my conversations with a high-caste friend whose grandmother had been one of the last Balinese women to offer herself as a human sacrifice when her royal husband died. In the nineteenth century, it was common for royal wives and concubines to throw themselves into the king's funeral pyre, usually after being stabbed. My friend believed that he could feel the presence of the powerful spirit of his ancestress in the temple. She had become a being of great *sakti,* or spiritual power, and as head of his family he would go to the temple to encourage her continuing interest in the welfare of her descendants.

The *odalan* or major festival of the Pura Dalem is timed for the full moon, which gives enough light for people to see the performances held in the evening. The festival began quietly in the late afternoon, as married women arrived with their children, wearing elegant sarongs and carrying flower offerings on their heads as offerings to the gods. Later, they were joined by their husbands and older sons, and knelt together in family groups as the priests intoned prayers to Durga, the demonic female incarnation of the Hindu god Siwa, and other gods of this temple. Families came and went as the evening went on, but by about ten o'clock a crowd had gathered just outside the temple gates for a performance of Calon Arang, the "candidate witch." This performance belongs to the bebali (middle courtyard) genre but is held outside the temple because the drama spills over into the nearby graveyard. This was to be a special performance because the mask of the witch Rangda, which is ordinarily kept under a sacred white cloth in the temple, had recently been refurbished. Earlier, in preparation for the use of the Rangda mask in the drama, two major rituals had already been performed by a Brahmin high priest: the first when the mask was taken down and the spirit of the witch-goddess was invited to depart for a while so that her mask could be repaired and painted; and a second ritual, after the work was done, to invite the witch's spirit to return. The high priest's job was done when he had finished the necessary prayers. But had the mask regained its power?

On the night of the performance, the masks and costumes for the play were respectfully removed from the inner sanctum, after prayers to Durga by the priests and performers. Meanwhile, just outside the temple gates, members of the gamelan orchestra from one of the banjars brought out their instruments and seated themselves, awaiting the signal to begin. With the moon high enough overhead to illuminate the temple, the performance began with a couple of hapless peasants wandering across an imaginary battlefield, their dialogue indicating that they had just witnessed a battle between the army of King Erlangga and an angry witch. Essentially, this is a longer version of the Barong and Rangda story described earlier. But since the story is very well-known to the audience, the action quickly centered on an improvised scene in a graveyard, where the two buffoons had foolishly fallen asleep. As they doze, three witches emerge from the temple and begin to dig near them. Soon one of the witches triumphantly pulls the corpse of a human infant out of the ground. Their whoops of delight as they begin feeding on the corpse startle the sleepers, who wake up and begin to talk, disturbing the witches' feast. Two of the witches drop the baby's corpse and run a short distance away, but the largest and ugliest witch begins to tease one of the farmers, sneaking up on him as he begins to doze. Seeing the witch, the second farmer lets out a shriek of terror and runs away, never to be seen again. The witch continues to tease the sleeper, shaking her breasts and hips at him suggestively. Sleepily he grabs the witch from behind, but as he awakens he sees her and screams with

A Topeng dancer portraying a noble king

fright. The audience has been laughing uproariously though all this, but when the witch kills the farmer and begins to eat him the temple grows quiet. The two other witches now return, retrieving the corpse of the child to add to their feast.

Now the music changes, and two actors wearing the sacred mask and costume of the Barong emerge from the temple. As the Barong dances out of the gate and into the performance space, the three witches take fright and dash off, abandoning the bodies of the man and child. While the Barong stands guard over the bodies, a group of villagers dressed like members of the audience arrive and pick up the body of the man and child, which they carry away in the direction of the sea. The man and the doll are treated as though they are dead bodies until they receive real prayers and holy water from a waiting priest. Suddenly, from inside the temple we hear the shouted challenge of Rangda the witch. In the Calon Arang story, she is the witch who laid waste the kingdom of Erlangga in mythical times. But this Rangda is also the eternal Rangda who lurks in every temple of death. The audience jumps to its feet and watches as more cries and challenges are heard from the temple, and suddenly Rangda herself appears, accompanied by the other three witches and two human servants carrying gilded umbrellas above her head. The witches stand in the temple gate, and Rangda hurls challenges—at the audience? King Erlangga? the Barong?—as she waves a magical white cloth that can make her invisible. The Barong begins to lunge forward and snap its jaws, when suddenly the actor playing Rangda goes into a violent trance. Half a dozen people in the audience rush up to attack the witches, and several are handed knives, but they are driven back by Rangda's screams. The actor playing Rangda appears to go into violent convulsions, and then suddenly begins to run off across the graveyard, in the direction of the funeral party carrying the two corpses. The gamelan stops playing, since the performance has now ended. Priests rush off in pursuit of the witches, whom they eventually catch and revive with holy water. The mask of Rangda is returned to the temple, and everyone goes home to bed, satisfied that the mask of the witch has not lost its potency.

I think what makes performances like this grip the imagination of an audience who knows the story very well is the ever-present possibility of what we call "trance" or "possession." In bebalih performances, anyone may become "possessed" at any moment, though most often it occurs to some of the actors and actresses. Trance is unpredictable and possibly dangerous, because it allows supernatural beings like witches to temporarily occupy a human body. But it also establishes a moment of contact between the members of the congregation and the unseen world. If possible, persons still in trance are brought into the inner sanctum of the temple and encouraged to speak—or rather, the supernatural beings that have taken control of them are invited to describe their wishes, just as trance mediums (balian ketakson) are asked to go into trance to seek the causes of illness or misfortune.

CONCLUSION: ART AND BALINESE CULTURE

Performances like the one described above are obviously far more than entertainment. In my dissertation, I argued that they played a key role in the process that historians term *Indianization:* the spread of Indic customs and institutions like the caste system, kingship, literature, and the Hindu religion to Bali. This process must have begun many centuries ago, when Bali somehow came into contact with the centers of Indian culture. But it is also true that there has been no significant contact between Bali and India for more than a thousand years. What kept these ancient traditions alive for so many centuries on this Pacific island? I had begun trying to understand how Balinese culture supported the arts, but in the end I saw things the other way 'round:

> We are looking for the moments when a great civilization touched a small island, which we know resulted in the creation of a tiny but nonetheless quite spectacular civilization. Thus we are inclined to imagine a great procession of glorious Indian culture bearers winding their way across Java, over the mountains and across the sea to Bali. A great priest steps forth, several gods descend from Heaven, and in a magical moment, Balinese civilization is borne.
>
> But what really happened, if the picture presented by the real archaeological evidence is accurate, was perhaps even more magical. The heroes, gods and priests—the whole procession—did indeed reach Bali, but it did so through the arts and the imagination. Embedded in the old inscriptions and tax records, we find the record of their arrival: groups of artists who visited the courts and villages, conjuring the entire procession out of the air in their performances. The great procession of kings and priests did not arrive once, physically, but innumerable times in countless courts and villages. It is quite possible, even likely, that not a single Indian visited Bali between the fifth and fifteenth centuries, when Bali's civilization was coming into being. It is even more likely that no Balinese actually visited India. Indeed, the India that Indianized Bali—the India of Indra's heaven, of the epic poems, of Mount Meru—could not be found by sailing across an earthly ocean.[48]

NOTES

31. Margaret Mead, "The Arts in Bali," originally published in *The Yale Review,* Vol. XXX, No. 2 (December 1940):335–347; reprinted in Jane Belo, ed., *Traditional Balinese Culture.* New York: Columbia University Press, 1970.

32. Jane Belo, ed., *Traditional Balinese Culture,* xii.

33. Arthur Waley, Preface to Beryl de Zoete and Walter Spies, *Dance and Drama in Bali.* London: Faber and Faber, 1938, xix.

34. Paul Oskar Kristeller, "The Modern System of the Arts," in *Renaissance Thought II.* New York: Harper and Row, 1965, 226.

35. The Balinese term for letters is *aksara,* from the Sanskrit, meaning "indestructible," and connoting the foundation of all existence.

36. Most Balinese literature is written on the leaves of the lontar palm, which are cut into narrow rectangles and smoothed, so that letters can be incised with a small knife. Afterwards, black soot is rubbed over both sides of each leaf, creating beautiful letters. Both sides of each leaf are used, except for the outer leaf of the first page, which is left blank because it is exposed to wear. Lontar manuscripts are thought to survive for about a hundred years, so many Balinese manuscripts have been recopied many times since writing began in the first millenium A.D.

37. Sa is connected with samana, the ether or wind, which occupies the heart or center of a cosmological object, and appears as a bright light. Samana is associated with the god Iswara.

38. Balinese *bayu, sabda, hidep* ("action or energy," "speech," "thought"), which the *trikaya-parisuddha* define as the components of right action (dharma).

39. The mapping of specific letters to the parts of the body varies according to local custom and the purposes of the ritual, so that *Sa* is not always located beneath the heart. There are many different versions of the "cosmic map," associated with different gods, elements, etc.

40. *Alangö* is Kawi or Old Javanese; the Balinese equivalent is *langa*. However, literate Balinese would recognize langa as derived from the Kawi word. The noun form in Balinese is *kalangengang*, "beauty."

41. Kawi literature does not definitively identify the deity of alangö as either masculine or feminine, but Ida Bagus consistently referred to *alangö* as feminine.

42. "Literary Balinese" is High Balinese enriched with Old Javanese vocabulary, and may not be understood by speakers of ordinary Low Balinese.

43. Zoetmulder, Kalangwan, op.cit., 209.

44. Bebetin A1 (Goris 002): 2b. 4–5

45. Sixteen districts *(kecamatan)* in southern Bali kept statistical records on their population, amount of rice terraces, number of temples, and number of different types of performing art groups. Plotting the simple *r*-correlation among these variables yields a clear pattern in which the strongest correlation is between the number of temples and the number of art groups. This correlation is much stronger than the simple correlation of population to art groups, which I interpret as evidence that temples rather than sheer numbers of people are the major source of patronage for the arts.

The diagram below shows the Pearson's *r*-correlation between each pair of variables:

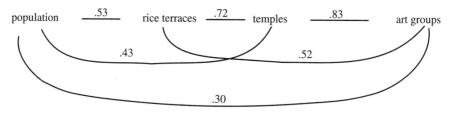

The four variables form a Markov chain in which each variable is most closely linked to the variables closest to it in the chain. The correlation weakens to more distant variables. For an extended discussion of these results, see Lansing 1983:65–74.

46. Some small temples lack a middle courtyard. In such cases the intermediate zone of bebalih performances is simply the middle of the temple, wherever that may be.

47. The outer gate to the temple is symbolically significant, because it marks the boundary between the world with all its corruptions and the sacred realm inside. Here, at the beginning of most temple festivals, there are cockfights or blood sacrifices to the demonic or elemental powers, the buta kala.

48. Lansing, *The Three Worlds of Bali*. New York: Praeger, 1983:29.

4 / The Goddess
and the Green Revolution

INTRODUCTION

The village of Sukawati lies between two rivers, the Oos and the Petanu. Between the village and the sea, there is a large block of about five hundred hectares of rice terraces that keeps over a thousand Sukawati farmers busy, wet rice being the world's most labor-intensive crop. On the last little knoll before the beach, where the rice terraces end, there is a magnificent old temple called the Masceti Er Jeruk. I became interested in this temple during my fieldwork in Sukawati in 1975. But while I wanted to learn about the legendary history of the temple, the local farmers were more interested in talking about its current problems. I learned that in the old days the temple had set an irrigation schedule for all the rice terraces in its vicinity. But as a result of a new agricultural policy called the Green Revolution, the temple had lost control of the irrigation schedule, and everyone was planting rice as often as they could, without regard for the temple's irrigation schedules.

The term "Green Revolution" refers to the replacement of native rice with specially bred high-yielding varieties (HYVs), which require the use of chemical fertilizers and pesticides. The Green Revolution began in the laboratories of the International Rice Research Institute in the Philippines in the 1960s, and spread swiftly across Asia, gaining a firm foothold in Indonesia by the early 1970s. In Bali, the Green Revolution was accompanied by new government agricultural policies, which promoted continuous cropping of the new HYV rice in an effort to boost rice production. With a fast-growing population, government planners were eager to find new ways to increase agricultural yields, and farmers were encouraged to plant HYVs as often as possible. But in Bali, the immediate gains in rice yields soon began to be offset by water shortages and unprecedented outbreaks of rice pests and diseases. In Sukawati, the farmers were required to grow HYV rice continuously, which provided an uninterrupted source of food for all the local rice pests.

In 1979, I returned to Bali for two short trips connected with the making of a documentary film. I spent several weeks in Sukawati, and learned that the old temple had managed to regain control of the irrigation schedules. The farmers had decided that the policy of continuous rice cropping had failed to increase harvests, because it made the water supply too unpredictable and led to increasing losses from pests. But policy makers were still pushing the Green Revolution, and there was a political struggle going on between "conservative" farmers who preferred to return to the old system of irrigation management by temples, and those who wanted to grow rice as often as possible.

In 1983 I returned with my family for a year to study the role of temples like Er Jeruk in the ecology of rice production. It seemed to me that there was an urgent need for a better understanding of how the traditional Balinese system worked, before it was too late. Some rice terraces in Bali are at least a thousand years old, and have produced one or two crops every year, year after year, century after century. In fact, rice terraces are the most ecologically stable and productive agricultural system ever invented, capable of supporting a large population indefinitely. Were modern development planners right to think that the water temples had outlived their usefulness?

We lived in a sort of bungalow in the rice paddies near the village of Kedewatan. The house belonged to the head of a *subak,* or farmer's association, named Wayan. Subaks are associations of farmers who share the water from a single source, like a spring or an irrigation canal. They have both practical and religious functions pertaining to water management and rice cultivation. Wayan's subak encompassed 133 hectares of terraces, owned by about double that number of farmers. The house we rented from Wayan was located not in the village but in the midst of his fields, making it easy to observe both rice-field rituals and farming activities. It was also conveniently located to observe seasonal changes in the insect population of the paddies: my wife's open-air kitchen always had a fair selection. Another good indicator of the pest populations in the rice paddies was the number of bats that turned up at sundown to catch airborne insects.

My research strategy was quite simple: I spent hours with Wayan, trying to observe every detail of what went on in his fields, asking endless questions about what I saw, and following him on his errands connected with both the "practical" and the "religious" aspects of rice production. In the evenings, my wife and I compared my observations with those of several other scholars: a German named Paul Wirz, who published a superb study of Balinese agriculture and the "rice cult" in 1927; the Dutch colonial administrators V. E. Korn, F. A. Liefrinck, and Charles Grader; the more recent work of an American anthropologist, Clifford Geertz; and a thoughtful critique of Geertz's ideas by an English anthropologist, Mark Hobart. I mention the names of these scholars here because their work was the starting point for my project. The basic issue was the relationship between the practical role of the subak in rice-terrace ecology and the rituals of the "rice cult." As subak head, Wayan had to organize both activities for the members of his subak: the intricate series of rituals of the "rice cult," which were carried out in the fields and local temples; and the actual physical work in the paddies, from field preparation to harvest. Earlier, Clifford Geertz had proposed an elegant model of the relationship between these two tasks, showing that the timing of the ceremonies of the rice cult is "symbolically linked to cultivation in a way that locks the pace of that cultivation into a firm, explicit rhythm." The "water-opening ceremony," for example, actually marks the beginning of the irrigation schedule, just as the harvest ceremonies mark its end. The rituals of the rice cult thus provide a way for the farmers to time the flow of water and the phases of agricultural labor. In Bali, Geertz wrote, "a complex ecological order was both reflected in and shaped by an equally complex ritual order, which at once grew out of it and was imposed upon it."[49]

But another anthropologist, Mark Hobart, found that the actual sequence of rituals is often badly synchronized with what is happening in the fields. He criticized Geertz for creating an idealized picture of the match between rituals and rice growth, and suggested that the real picture was far more complex.

Fortunately for me, the subak head I was working with became quite interested in this controversy. Wayan had already served as subak head for twenty-odd years, and was very knowledgeable about the workings of the subaks in his area. While he saw Geertz's point, he also believed that subak rituals served more important purposes than timekeeping. Wayan was also curious about the reasons for differences in the ritual cycles between subaks in different regions of Bali. We both suspected that they might be related to variations in ecological conditions. Wayan willingly agreed to visit other subaks with me, so we could compare the details of their ritual cycles with his. These journeys took us to many subaks and water temples, but the real turning point in the research came when I accompanied Wayan and a small delegation of farmers up to the Temple of the Crater Lake for an annual temple festival that draws together more than two hundred subaks.

I am going to begin the water temple story there, at the Temple of the Crater Lake, rather than with my first journeys with Wayan. It took quite a long time to make sense of the water temple system, and we don't have time here to retrace the whole story. Instead, by skipping ahead to the Temple and the Goddess of the Lake, we can begin this chapter in a more Balinese way, at the center of yet another "cosmological map."

THE GODDESS OF THE LAKE AND HER TEMPLE

From anywhere in central Bali, a farmer need only glance up to the clouds around Mount Batur to be reminded of the ultimate origin of the water flowing into his fields. In the crater of the volcano, at an elevation well above the height at which rice may be grown, there is an immense fresh-water lake, stretching over 4,240 acres.[50] The lake is regarded by the farmers and temple priests as the ultimate source of water for the rivers and springs that provide irrigation water for the whole of central Bali. Priests describe the mountain lake as a sacred mandala, or cosmic map of waters, fed by springs lying at each of the wind directions, high above the irrigated lands. The steam from the caldera of Mount Batur represents the zenith of the mandala, while the nadir is found in the depths of the lake. Each of the springs around the lake is regarded as the origin of waters for a particular hydrological region of central Bali.

The entire mandala of the lake forms the center of a much larger mandala, consisting of the island of Bali and the seas that surround it. Priests sometimes speak of the lake as a freshwater ocean, filled with life-giving water, which contrasts with the salt ocean that encircles it, far below. The lake is the home of one of the two supreme deities of Bali, the "Goddess of the Lake," Dewi Danu. Her relationship to the farmers of central Bali is succinctly defined in a manuscript kept in her temple:

"... because the Goddess makes the waters flow, those who do not follow her laws may not possess her rice terraces."[51]

According to legend, the goddess and her male counterpart, the God of Mount Agung, emerged from an erupting volcano in the year 231 (on our calendar). Together with other, lesser gods, they took possession of the land and waters of Bali. The goddess rules the lake and Mount Batur, the second-highest peak in Bali, while the god rules Mount Agung. As the male and female deities of the two highest mountains, they form a complementary pair, the supreme gods of the island. The male god of Mount Agung is worshipped at the temple of Besakih, high on Mount Agung, and is symbolically associated with the king of Klungkung, who claims supremacy over all other Balinese kings. But the Goddess of the Lake has no special relationship to any king or kingdom. Her principal congregation consists of several hundred subaks, which make annual pilgrimages to her mountain-top temple called Pura Ulun Danu Batur, the Temple of the Crater Lake.

When I began my research, the Temple of the Crater Lake's relationship to the subaks was not described in the literature on Balinese religion or water management. Yet the importance of the temple for the farmers can be detected in some of the earliest descriptions of Bali by foreign visitors. For example, in 1830 a missionary traveler was sent to Bali by the Singapore Christian Union to explore the prospects for "extending the benefits of Education and the knowledge of Christianity" to the Balinese. At that time, very little was known about Balinese culture. The missionary's report begins with a brief list of the principal Balinese courts, after which he turns his attention to the "riches of Bali":

> Bali has several inland lakes or reservoirs of water situated near the tops of high mountains, several thousand feet above the level of the sea. These lakes all contain fresh water, whose rise and fall corresponds to the sea. Their depths are great, but irregular: in some parts bottom has been found at forty or fifty fathoms and in other parts it is said no bottom can be got at the depth of several hundred fathoms. Some of them are long, and others round, the largest about four miles across, and twelve in circumference; at any rate, they contain water enough to irrigate the inhabited parts of the island with little trouble and expense; and however much water is taken from them, they never seem to decrease. These lakes form the riches of Bali; in a country where there are no great rivers, and where the inhabitants have to depend for subsistence entirely on the irrigation of their rice fields, these lakes are indispensable, and without them it appears evident that so great a population could not be maintained. The scarcity of waters elsewhere is so great, and all the rivers so insignificant, that persons traveling in the dry season are obliged to carry water with them, but by means of these lakes the diligent husbandman is enabled to obtain water enough for all his wants, and consequently two crops of rice are taken annually . . . [52]

Interestingly, the missionary got his facts wrong, but in such a way as to confirm the myth. The lakes do not have tides, of course, nor do they have river outlets. But in temple rituals the crater lake is described as an ocean, a metaphysical idea that the missionary evidently took literally. It is also part of the mythology of the temple that the lakes are connected to the rivers by underground tunnels. The water in the lakes is thought to pour out continuously through these tunnels, yet "however much water is taken from them, they never seem to decrease." This belief in underground tunnels from the crater lakes as the source of irrigation waters was also mentioned in a report by a Dutch colonial officer in 1887:

There are temples by the shore of every lake in Bali, for it is believed that the streams are fed from the lakes by underground tributaries. Yearly pilgrimages must be made to these sanctuaries . . . [53]

At the time of my fieldwork, a hundred years later, these yearly pilgrimages continued, as thousands of farmers brought offerings to the Goddess of the Lake in appreciation for her gift of water.

The temple used to be located down in the crater, between the still-active caldera and the lake. A volcanic eruption brought a towering river of lava to within a few feet of the temple's gate, as can be seen in a photograph taken a few years later. A Dutch architect who visited the temple in 1918 was amazed, writing that

> The fame of holiness, coming from this temple, has risen after the last eruption of Batoer in 1905 even more by the miraculous way by which it was then saved from total destruction. The glowing lava stream was stopped just at the main entrance in an inexplicable way![54]

But in August 1926, the old temple was not so lucky. The Dutch officer in charge of the district reported what happened:

> On the third of August 1926, at 1 A.M., Mount Batur began to erupt. Along the north-western slope a long crevice appeared with a lot of noise and thunder, from which fires and many lava fountains spewed forth. I was informed of this and went to Kintamani, and descended to the village of Batur. It was impossible to get an overview of the situation: the inhabitants were not worried, and trusted in the power and will of the gods, and in the temple which already once before had stopped the lava-stream. From above you

Baris Gde (warrior) dancers in front of the Temple of the Crater Lake (Pura Ulun Danu Batur) before the 1917 earthquake. Note the wall of lava that stopped just outside the gate. Archives of the KITLV, Leiden.

could see that the lava-stream was not moving towards the village. However, it seemed to me that the continuous eruptions would eventually fill the hollow in which the village was nestled. In the afternoon of the first day a new source of lava came into being at about 1,200 meters distance from the village. With the sound of a diesel engine, it regularly emitted large waves of blood-red glowing lava. A lava stream started to move towards the village . . .[55]

The village and the temple were quickly abandoned, as the inhabitants raced for safety. A new temple was soon constructed on the rim of the crater, looking down on the great lake and the still-active caldera.

I first visited the temple in the company of Wayan and half a dozen farmers from his subak, in February 1984. We arrived in two small trucks and unloaded the subak's offerings: a live pig, half a truckload of coconuts, some live chickens, and many baskets of unhulled rice. These were hauled away to pens and storerooms behind the kitchens, while we were given a meal. I learned that unlike other Balinese temples, the Temple of the Crater Lake is always manned by a small staff of priests and elders, who are always available to welcome visitors (usually subaks experiencing problems with water shortages or rice pests). A few days later, I returned to the temple with a much larger delegation consisting of about forty people from Wayan's subak. They brought their own individual offerings to the goddess, which they placed before the altars in the inner sanctum of the temple. Priests guided them in prayers, sprinkled everyone with holy water from the lake, and presented the leaders of the subak with a bamboo tube filled with holy water. This water was taken home to the subak's main temple, there to be mixed with more holy water and distributed to every family to sprinkle on their fields. Meanwhile, the temple's ancient Great Orchestra (Gong Gde) played as dozens more subaks arrived. After making their offerings and receiving their holy water, most subaks exited via the kitchens, where all the farmers were given a cooked meal by the temple staff. The ingredients for these meals came from the temple's storerooms, from offerings like those Wayan's subak had brought up a few weeks earlier. With an active congregation of more than two hundred subaks, the temple is able to feed thousands of people during major festivals.

The Temple of the Crater Lake was clearly key to understanding the water temple system, and in the past ten years I have spent many months at the temple or on journeys with its priests. My vantage point on the subaks gradually shifted from my wife's kitchen overlooking Wayan's fields to the kitchens adjoining the temple's storerooms. This proved to be an ideal place to learn about how subaks handle problems or disputes. The temple kitchens are continuously manned on a regular schedule by teams of priests and elders. When a subak delegation arrives, they are first led into the kitchens, where they are offered food and drink, and given a chance to describe the reason for their visit to the temple. I could listen in, ask questions, and try to follow up the most interesting cases, often with the help of temple priests.

There are twenty-four permanent priests of the temple, who are chosen in childhood as lifelong servants of the goddess. This priesthood is organized in a hierarchy, and at its summit there is a single high priest who is believed to be the earthly representative of the Goddess of the Lake. This priest is called the Jero Gde. He is also known as Sanglingan, "Lightning-struck," because he is selected in childhood by a virgin priestess[56] of the temple, after the death of his predecessor. On these occasions, the priestess goes into trance to allow the Goddess of the Lake to possess her voice and describe the boy whom she has chosen to become the new Jero Gde. From the moment of his selection until the day of his death, the Jero Gde is regarded as the earthly representative of the Goddess of the Lake. By day he offers sacrifices to her on behalf of the hundreds of subaks that make up the temple's principal congregation. By night, he may receive guidance from her in dreams. He is always dressed in white, the color of purity, and wears his hair long. Although he is of commoner caste, his permanent identification with the Goddess of the Lake sets him apart from all other Balinese priests.

It is true that other priests are sometimes believed to be possessed by a deity. For example, at the climax of the ritual for creating holy water, Brahmana high priests[57] are thought to incarnate the god Siwa. Similarly, trance mediums (*balian*) are regularly "possessed" by unseen spirits. But in these cases, when the ritual or trance is finished, the link between priests and deities is broken. In contrast, the magical identification of the Jero Gde with the Goddess of the Lake continues for his lifetime. In the case of the current Jero Gde, it is said that signs of his special relationship with the goddess were detected even before he was chosen. As he explained to me:

"... Before I was chosen, I had a feeling—a strangeness in myself. I mean, often when I went home, I was given a name alluding to the presence of a god."

Once, I asked him what it was like for an eleven-year-old boy to suddenly take on the responsibilities of a Jero Gde. His answer stressed the guiding role of the goddess:

"... the Deity chose me through the trance of the Virgin Priestess. Then I immediately went through the ceremonies of 'installation'—I was purified, to become the Jero Gde. At that time I was still eleven years old . . . But because I was selected by an imperial Deity (Ida Sasuunan), there were no problems. I simply went along, just as I do now. I had become the Jero Gde, even if I was still a child."

While ordinary Balinese priests are not identified in this way with deities, kings are. According to Balinese religious belief, the Goddess of the Lake and the God of Mount Agung share dominion over the island, a concept that is taken literally by the inhabitants of the mountains, who point to the side of the lake where the power of the goddess stops and the dominion of the god begins. In the time before the Dutch, when Bali was ruled by kings, the king of Bali was symbolically identified with the male God of Mount Agung and Besakih temple. But while the powers of the king of Bali derived from his descent, those of the Jero Gde originate in the logic of the water temple system. Unlike the king, who claimed symbolic dominion over the whole of Bali, the authority of the Jero Gde is strictly limited. As the living representative of the Goddess of the Lake, his powers extend to the Temple of the Crater Lake and the waters believed to originate from the lake. Essentially, he is a temple priest, but his relationship to the Goddess of the Lake gives him a special authority over irrigation water. As he himself remarked,

"... it is only the Goddess of the Lake who can properly give water. She already embodies, incarnates water, which she gives to her subaks, from the lake . . ."

But did the symbolic identification of the Jero Gde with his goddess endow him with real control over water rights? Or was his position purely symbolic? One afternoon I put this question to a subak head. This was his response:

SUBAK HEAD: It's like this. Everything that concerns the subaks is interconnected. The word is *anugraha* ("grant" or "gift"). So that—as with the fifteen subaks located at our Masceti temple—the flow from the spring has been calculated. It produces enough for so many hectares. Now if, for example, there was a request for more water, obviously the Jero Gde must lower his hand, give a decision. So it won't happen that those who have received the "grant"—from the Masceti temple and the Batur temple—don't get enough water. Because they have the right, from earlier times. Because these things are usually written in the records at the Temple of the Crater Lake.

This answer appeared to affirm the authority of the Jero Gde over the allocation of water rights. But I wondered whether the priest merely gave his blessing to whatever decision had been taken by the farmers. Had he ever refused a request for irrigation water?

SUBAK HEAD: Earlier, there was a request to open new terraces here—a request that went straight to the Temple of the Crater Lake. But, well, maybe because the Jero Gde was concerned about the people of my village, anyway he didn't give permission. If he had, there would have been a lot of twists and turns! So it was dropped. Up till now, it hasn't happened. The water can't be taken.

We, too, once had a desire to open new lands, convert some dry fields to rice terraces. We asked permission from the Temple of the Crater Lake, so that our water would be sufficient for the new terraces. But the Jero Gde declined.

LANSING: Where . . . ?

SUBAK HEAD: Just upstream from the Bayad weir, we wanted to use that water. There is a spring there; we wanted to use it. We weren't going to build a new weir on the river, just use that spring. But if we did, the Bayad weir would have been affected (i.e., there would be a reduction in the flow reaching the Bayad weir). So we had to abandon the idea.

LANSING: Where does the authority of the Jero Gde come from?

SUBAK HEAD: Belief . . . overflowing belief. Concerning Batur temple—really that is the center, the origin of waters, you see. At this moment, the Jero Gde holds all this in his hands. At the Temple of Lake Batur.

This answer was in accord with the image of the role of the Jero Gde and the mandala of waters described by the temple priests. Evidently, the subaks acknowledged the right of the Jero Gde to decide upon water allocations, in the name of the goddess. But to truly resolve the question of the extent of the temple's authority over water rights, I sought out cases that involved real disputes. I soon found a good one: a case in which a subak tore apart the dam belonging to their upstream neighbors.

A QUARREL BETWEEN SUBAKS

The village of Pengalu lies at high elevation, and began growing rice on irrigated terraces only ten years ago. Formerly they relied on rainfall to grow dry rice and vegetable crops. In 1986, the village sent a messenger to urgently request a visit from the Jero Gde. In response, the Jero Gde sent a temple messenger to inquire into the case. I spoke to the messenger, who described the problem as follows:

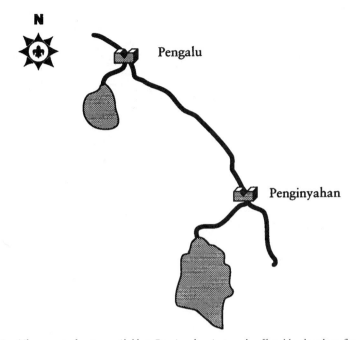

Figure 12   *The amount of water available to Penginyahan is strongly affected by the release flow from Pengalu.*

TEMPLE MESSENGER: It had to do with water. The source was a little to the north of the village of Pengalu, to the northwest. The water was taken by Pengalu, and brought down. Earlier, there was enough. But now, in the dry season, there wasn't enough for Penginyahan (the village immediately downstream from Pengalu). So this became a problem. The water for Pengalu—the new subak—was taken back by Penginyahan.

On the appointed date, I drove to the village with the Jero Gde and a delegation from the temple. By observing what he said and did, I hoped to be able to gauge the extent of his real powers over irrigation. We were accompanied by two temple messengers who are responsible for this region of central Bali, and two of the regular priests of the Temple of the Crater Lake.

When we arrived at the village of Pengalu, the entire subak was seated in their village meeting hall, awaiting our arrival. We were led to seats on an elevated platform, where four village leaders joined us facing the subak. I requested permission to tape the meeting, and the Jero Gde nodded his acknowledgment. Rather nervously, the village leaders agreed. After brief welcoming remarks, the head of the subak explained the problem:

SUBAK HEAD:. . . so we built a weir on the Telaga Genteg stream. The weir was built by the whole community. The idea was to raise the waters to irrigate terraces for the hamlets of Kerta and Mawang. . . . A little while ago, if I'm not mistaken, on the 21st and 22nd of January, our subak was demolished by subak Penginyahan. Why the people of Penginyahan wrecked our weir,[58] we don't know. So since the 22nd of January, 1986, we of subak Pengalu haven't had water. No water at all enters subak Pengalu. There were about two hundred people from Penginyahan, led by the heads of their subak and village. The government—the police, *kabupaten* and *kecamatan*[59]—have taken this in hand, but nothing has been done. So that you may know, Jero Gde, that this is how things are for subak Pengalu. Our subak is ten years old, we have harvested rice for ten years, and we have joined the congregation of the Temple of Batur. Now Penginyahan has engaged in destruction. So subak Pengalu up to now hasn't planted rice. Our fields are empty. . . .

JERO GDE: In these things, if we find a path the way we do in Bali, there is only one (way), which is the direction upstream, to the origins. Isn't it so? Who is the owner of these waters? In truth, when matters develop into a big confrontation, everyone's wishes are bad, then everything turns bad. And the effect is, the water is not used. Water that is needed. So it is. So this new problem, first I must take it up to the regent (*bupati*). Such things, every aspect must be taken up or they can't be concluded. Now apparently this forest area is only producing about a hundred liters of water, right?[60] If things don't work out, that water is definitely wasted. Lost, useless. My concern is, I don't promise, but let us together make strenuous efforts, force things into the very best path, then perhaps we can obtain the opportunity to fix this situation of ours, our dam at Pengalu. May the village easily receive this path, which is my decree, so that the path you've begun with the bupati can be followed to the end. Together!

After these remarks, the Jero Gde asked to visit the site of the damaged weir. The entire structure had been washed away, and the river was flowing freely in the direction of Penginyahan, a few kilometers downstream. After looking the situation over, the Jero Gde asked the subak to gather around him, and addressed them:

JERO GDE: I am ready to add to my former words. As I asked earlier, who owns these waters? Clearly it is only the Deities who prevent this spring from drying up, is it not so? What about downstream? Now you of Pengalu already have the right to use some of this water. And for those below (i.e., the Penginyahan irrigation system) there was no shortage, formerly? For Pengalu here, just how many hectares were in use before the dam was destroyed?

SUBAK HEAD: About thirty hectares.

JERO GDE: So now, my wishes are, remember the Goddess! Things are not good now, so the medicine must be applied quickly. As for me, I feel very sad. Together, then, let's begin.

THE COSMOLOGICAL ROLE OF WATER TEMPLES

The Temple of the Crater Lake sits high on the rim of the crater above Lake Batur. Symbolically, it is situated at the center of a mandala, or cosmic map, that encompasses the whole of the island of Bali. This cosmological map has a meaningful structure, based on the idea that the Goddess of the Lake brings life to the fields and villages by causing the rivers and springs to flow down the sides of the volcano. Wherever a group of farmers divert some of the waters of the goddess into their fields, they construct a temple or a shrine where they can show their gratitude with prayers and offerings. The larger temples also provide a place for farmers to meet and talk over practical problems, such as irrigation schedules. However, the practical role of the water temples in ecosystem management makes sense only in the context of their "cosmological" meaning.

Each of the hundreds of small-scale irrigation systems along Balinese rivers begins with a spring or, more often, a weir (diversionary dam) in a river, which diverts all or part of the flow into an irrigation canal. Beside each weir or spring there is always a small shrine or temple, where the farmers who benefit from this particular flow of water can make offerings to the Goddess of the Lake and the "Deity of the Weir" (*Bhatara Empelan*), who are thought to make the waters flow into the canal.

The irrigation canal, which takes off from the weir, eventually reaches a block of terraces. This spot is usually a kilometer or more downstream from the weir and is marked by a major water temple, the "Head of the Rice Terraces Temple" (Pura Ulun Swi). The congregation of this temple is the same as that of the weir shrine: it consists of all farmers who grow rice in the terraces irrigated by this particular canal system. The principal deity of the Ulun Swi Temple is called Ida Bhatara Pura Ulun Swi, the "Deity of the Ulun Swi Temple," whose influence extends to all of the terraces watered by the canal. The temple itself is simply a walled courtyard containing a shrine where farmers can make offerings to this deity. Additional shrines provide a place for offerings to other gods and goddesses such as the Deity of the Weir and the Goddess of the Temple of the Crater Lake. These offerings at the Ulun Swi temple acknowledge the dependency of farmers on the flow of waters into their terraces, which in turn depends upon the flow at the weir, and ultimately upon the flow in the river.

Other water temples and shrines follow a similar logic. All water temples are physically located at the upstream edge of whatever water system they purport to control. Chains of water temples articulate the hydro-logic of each irrigation system. Temples and shrines are situated in such a way as to exert influence over each of the major physical components of the terrace ecosystems, including lakes, springs, rivers, weirs, major canals, blocks of irrigated terraces, subaks, and individual fields. The temples link these physical features of the landscape to social units according to a simple logic of production: the congregation of each temple consists of the farmers who obtain water from the irrigation component "controlled" by the temple's god.

Looking at the system from the bottom up, each farmer has a small shrine (*bedugul*) located at the spot where irrigation water first enters his fields. This "upstream" corner of his fields is considered sacred; it is here that he makes offerings to the Rice Goddess incarnate in his crop. At harvest time, the rice that grows closest to the water inlet is used to create a sacred image of the Rice Goddess herself, which is not eaten but carried to the rice barn and given offerings.

Upstream from the farmer's field shrine, the next water temple is usually the subak temple, representing a block of irrigated terraces with a common water source. Several subaks make up the congregation of an Ulun Swi temple, associated with a large canal, and a weir or spring shrine. Several weirs' subaks typically form the congregation of a *Masceti,* a regional water temple. Finally, each spring, lake, and the headwaters of each river have shrines or temples. The largest water temple is farthest upstream: the Temple of the Crater Lake, associated with Lake Batur, which is considered to be the source of all irrigation waters within its river boundaries.[61]

There are also important temples located at the downstream terminus of irrigation systems, which are classified as Masceti regional water temples. Upstream and

A water temple located in Lake Bratan

downstream temples have very different functions, associated with two different symbolic properties of water. Upstream water is associated with the nourishing or life-giving effects of water, and is regarded as a gift from the Goddess of the Lake. In contrast, downstream water is cleansing water: water used to purify, to wash away pollution. It is not collected in sacred vessels, like upstream water, but left running in the rivers. Impurities such as the ashes from sacrifices are thrown directly into the rivers, which bear them to the sea. This is the basis of a powerful symbolic contrast: while the waters high above in the crater lake represent the mystery of water as life-giver, the waters of the sea are associated with the equally potent mysteries of dissolution and regeneration. "Downstream" masceti temples are located at the downstream edge of the last block of rice terraces irrigated by major rivers, along the sea coast. By the time they reach the sea, the rivers are considered to be brimming with impurities: the ashes of burnt sacrifices, the discharge from villages and fields. The sea dissolves them all, removing their human content as impurities, and returning them to a wild, elemental, natural state.

ECOLOGY OF THE RICE TERRACES

But what is the relationship between the symbolic logic of water temple rituals and the actual practical ecology of the rice terraces? To answer this question, we need to understand something about the ecology of rice paddies.

There is no question that the rice terraces of Bali are quite ancient. One of the earliest known writings in the Balinese language, a royal edict from the eighth century A.D., refers not only to rice harvests but to irrigation-tunnel builders.[62] The oldest human settlements in Bali are concentrated in the best rice-growing areas, where it appears that some terraces have been under continuous cultivation for a millennium or more. Traditional rice paddies are unique in that they are able to produce large amounts of grain indefinitely, with no diminution in yields. By contrast, all other systems of irrigated agriculture are subject to a gradual decline in productivity as a consequence of salinization and loss of soil fertility.

As we have seen, most Balinese irrigation systems begin at a weir (diversionary dam) across a river, which diverts part of the flow into a tunnel. The tunnel may emerge as much as a kilometer or more downstream, at a lower elevation, where the water is routed through a system of canals and aqueducts to the summit of a terraced hillside. In the regions where rice cultivation is oldest in Bali, irrigation systems can be extraordinarily complex, with a maze of tunnels and canals shunting water through blocks of rice terraces. Since the volume of water in the rivers during the wet season can be ten times greater than the dry-season flow, the irrigation system has to cope with conditions ranging from a trickle to flash floods. Irrigation systems originating at different weirs are often interconnected, so that unused water from the tail end of one irrigation system may be shunted into a different block of terraces, or returned to a neighboring stream.

To appreciate the level of precision required for the system to work, it is necessary to understand something about the basic dynamics of the paddy ecosystem. In essence, the flow of water—the planned alternation of wet and dry phases—governs the basic biochemical processes of the terrace ecosystem. There is a general theory in ecology that holds that ecosystems characterized by steady, unchanging nutrient flows tend to be less productive than systems in which there are nutrient cycles or "pulses."[63] Rice paddies are an excellent example of this principle. Controlled changes in water levels create "pulses" in several important biochemical cycles. The cycle of wet and dry phases alters soil pH; induces a cycle of aerobic and anaerobic conditions in the soil, which determines the activity of microorganisms; circulates mineral nutrients; fosters the growth of nitrogen-fixing algae; excludes weeds; stabilizes soil temperature; and, over the long term, governs the formation of a plough pan that prevents nutrients from being leached into the sub-soil. Potassium, for example, is needed for the growth of the rice and depends largely on drainage. Phosphorus is also essential. It is slowly leached from the volcanic rock and transported by the rivers and irrigation canals. For this reason, phosphorus levels may be increased more than tenfold by regularly flooding the fields.[64]

The main crop produced is of course rice. But in addition, the paddy also produces important sources of animal protein such as eels, frogs, and fish. Even the dragonflies that gather over the rice to hunt insects are themselves hunted by little boys, who roast and eat them. Most paddies support a large population of ducks, which must also be carefully managed since they will damage young rice plants if left untended. After each harvest, flocks of ducks are driven from field to field, gleaning leftover grain and also eating some of the insects, like brown planthoppers, which would otherwise attack the next rice crop. Traditional harvesting techniques remove only the seed-bearing tassel, leaving the rest of the stalk to decompose in the water, returning most of its nutrients to the system. Depending upon the danger from

Rice terraces

rice pests, after harvesting, the farmer may decide to dry the field and burn the stalks, thus killing most pests but losing some of the nutrients in the harvested plants. Alternatively, he may flood the field and allow the rice stalks to slowly decompose under water.

As a method of pest control, the effectiveness of drying or flooding the fields depends on cooperation among all of the farmers in a given block of terraces. It would be useless for a single farmer to try to reduce the pests on his own field without coordinating with his neighbors, since the pests would simply migrate from field to field. But if all of the fields in a large area are burned or flooded, pest populations can be sharply reduced. Both kinds of fallow periods—burnt fields or flooded—are effective techniques for reducing the population of rice pests, but both depend on synchronizing the harvest and subsequent fallow period over a sufficiently large area. How many hectares must be left fallow, and for how long, depends on the species characteristics of the rice pests. Major pests include rodents, insects, and bacterial and viral diseases.

Just as individual farmers manage their paddies by controlling the flow of water, so larger social groups control pest cycles by means of synchronized irrigation schedules. The role of water in the microecology of the paddy—creating resource pulses—is duplicated on a larger scale by irrigation cycles that control pest populations by flooding or draining large blocks of terraces.

A good example of the practical role of water temples is provided by the largest water temple in my old village of Sukawati, the masceti temple Er Jeruk. Here the role of the temple is described by the head of the village, who is also a farmer:

VILLAGE HEAD: The Pura Er Jeruk is the largest temple hereabouts, that is, the temple whose congregation includes all the farmers of the village of Sukawati. Now below this temple there are also smaller temples, which are special places of worship for the subaks—each subak has its own. There are fourteen of these temples, fourteen subaks, all of which meet together as one here. They meet at the Temple Er Jeruk. Every decision, every rule concerning planting seasons and so forth, is always discussed here. Then, after the meeting here, decisions are carried down to each subak. The subaks each call all their members together: "In accord with the meetings we held at the Temple Er Jeruk, we must fix our planting dates, beginning on day one through day ten." For example, first subak Sango plants, then subak Somi, beginning from day ten through day twenty. Thus it is arranged, in accordance with water and "Padewasan"—that is, the best times to plant. Because here time controls everything. If there are many rodents and we go ahead and plant rice, obviously we'll get a miserable harvest. So we organize things like this: when the rodent population is large, we see to it that we don't plant things they can eat, so that they will all die—I mean, actually, that their numbers will be greatly reduced, pretty quickly . . .

LANSING: Is there a fixed schedule of meetings?

VILLAGE HEAD: Once a year. Each new planting season, there is a meeting. If the planting schedule is not to be changed, there is no meeting. Of course, the ceremonies held here go on regardless; there are two temple festivals here, a one-day festival every six months, and a three-day festival every year . . . This place is the home of the spirits of those who have preceded us, who built this temple. I would call this temple the fortress of the farmers hereabouts.

All three groups plant rice at least once a year, in the rainy season. During the dry season, there is a rotational system. One group is guaranteed water for a second planting of rice, and one group plants a vegetable crop, receiving water once every five days. The third group will plant either rice or vegetables, depending on whether the amount of irrigation water is judged adequate for rice. By setting the cropping pattern and irrigation schedule, the masceti temple attempts to optimize water sharing, while establishing a widespread fallow period, so as to reduce pest infestations.

ECOLOGICAL CRISIS: THE GREEN REVOLUTION

In the mid-1970s, the advent of the Green Revolution in Bali put an end to the practical role of temples like Er Jeruk in the creation of cropping patterns. To the extent that planners took any notice at all of water temples, they were inclined to dismiss them as religious institutions that had no constructive role to play in the campaign to boost rice production. The result was an ecological crisis. To understand what happened, we need a brief overview of the Green Revolution in Bali.

The Green Revolution began in Asia at the International Rice Research Institute (IRRI) in the Philippines. In 1962, IRRI agronomists developed a new high-yielding variety of rice called IR-8, which matured in 125 days and produced 5,800 pounds of grain per acre on test plots. In the late 1960s, IR-8 and its successors reached Indonesia. At that time, Indonesia was forced to import nearly a million tons of rice per year from other nations to feed a growing population. The Indonesian government became an enthusiastic proponent of the Green Revolution, which promised to dramatically increase rice production. Since the IRRI rice was designed to be responsive to chemical fertilizers, it was necessary to provide farmers with access to fertilizers and pesticides, as well as the new seed stocks. In 1967, the Indonesian government invited a Swiss company, CIBA, to develop a system for furnishing these necessities to farmers. The new program was called BIMAS for Bimbingan Massal, or Massive Guidance. Despite initial failures of the BIMAS program to increase rice production, the government decided to invest heavily in a national program to achieve self-sufficiency in rice. This program was based on two components: government subsidies to reduce the cost of fertilizers and pesticides to the farmers, and extension of BIMAS (which the government took over in 1971) to all major rice-growing regions of Indonesia. In order to ensure that farmers would have access to the fertilizers and pesticides required to grow the new "miracle rice," a government banking system (the People's Bank) was empowered to provide credit to small farmers for the specific purpose of purchasing agrochemicals and farm machinery. Massive Guidance brought rapid results: by 1974, 48 percent of the terraces of south-central Bali were planted with the new rice; three years later the proportion had climbed to 70 percent.[65]

Within a few years of the beginning of the Green Revolution, the government took two further steps that had a profound impact on the water temple system in Bali. The first was a shift in cropping patterns. IR-8 proved to be highly susceptible to an insect called the brown planthopper, which is estimated to have destroyed 2 million tons of rice in Indonesia in 1977. Rice scientists at IRRI came up with a new variety of rice, IR-36, which was resistant to the planthoppers and had the further advantage of maturing very quickly.[66] In Bali, the use of IR-36 was strongly encouraged. Balinese farmers were forbidden to plant native varieties, which take much longer to mature, are less responsive to fertilizers, and produce less grain. Instead, double-cropping or triple-cropping of IR-36 (or other high-yielding rice varieties) was legally mandated. Farmers were instructed to abandon the traditional cropping patterns and to plant high-yielding varieties as often as possible.

The second step was taken as a result of a series of studies by foreign consultants on ways to improve the performance of Balinese irrigation systems. These studies culminated in the Bali Irrigation Project, a major engineering project launched in 1979 by the Asian Development Bank. The aims of the project were succinctly defined in their feasibility study:[67]

> The Bali Irrigation Project (B.I.P.) is the first large scale attempt in Bali island to improve the irrigation systems. Past interventions by the Department of Public Works have been limited to isolated improvements, with negligible external consequences. In contrast, the B.I.P. will intervene in 130 subaks (about 10 percent of the total Bali subaks), many sharing the water from the same river. The impact of the main improvements will concern:
>
> River water sharing and subak coordination
> New Operating & Maintenance rules
> Programmed cropping patterns
> Use of measurement systems
> Changes in cropping techniques
> Yield monitoring systems
> Taxes and water charges
>
> In consequence the Subak may lose some of its traditional facets, especially part of its autonomy.

The principal emphasis of the project was the reconstruction of thirty-six weirs and associated irrigation works, at an estimated cost of about forty million dollars.[68] Since in most cases these "subak improvement schemes" were not designed to bring new land into cultivation, economic justification for the project was largely based on a mandated change to continuous rice cropping for as many subaks as possible. In the long run, according to project officials, this would generate a minimum of 80,000 tons of additional rice production each year, which could be sold for export and thus provide the $1,300,000 per annum needed to repay the Bali Irrigation Project loan to the Asian Development Bank.[69] All of these estimates were later revised upward, as the project added an additional sixteen subak improvement schemes to the original plan.

As a later evaluation report on the project noted, "The introduction of the project coincided with the government's push for self-sufficiency in rice and the encouragement given to farmers to extend the substitution of short rotation varieties [of rice] for the traditional long duration varieties. . . . These factors temporarily led to the abandonment of the Balinese cropping calendar, traditionally the key to overall watershed and irrigation scheme management."[70] By the late 1970s, the mandated change to continuous rice cropping began to remove the temples from control of irrigation and cropping patterns. In the upper reaches of the rivers, where coordination of irrigation was essential during the dry season, farmers often refused to abandon the temple schedules. But farther downstream, the threat of legal penalties against anyone failing to grow the new rice led to continuous cropping of Green Revolution rice. Religious rituals continued in the temples, but field rituals no longer matched the actual stages of rice growth. As soon as one crop was harvested, another was planted, and cropping cycles drifted apart. During the rainy season, no one was likely to run out of water. But during the dry season, the supply of irrigation water became unpredictable. Soon, district agricultural offices began to report "chaos in the water scheduling" and "explosions of pest populations," as in this 1985 report by the Department of Public Works of the Regency of Tabanan:

I. Background

Concerning the explosion of pests and diseases which recently attacked the rice crops, such as brown planthoppers, rodents, tungro virus, and other insects, in the Tabanan regency; and also with regard to the frequent problems which began to arise at about the same time concerning water sharing during the dry season, various groups are now urgently working to get on top of the problem. The result has been acknowledgment of the following factors which caused the explosion of pests and diseases:

1. In areas with sufficient irrigation water, farmers are now planting continuously throughout the year.

2. In areas with insufficient water, farmers are planting without a coordinated schedule.

In other words, the farmers/subaks have ceased to follow the centuries-old cyclical cropping patterns . . .

A similar report for the neighboring regency of Gianyar tells the same tale, beginning with the massive damage to crops caused by the brown planthopper in the late 1970s. As elsewhere in Bali, farmers in Gianyar were encouraged to plant the planthopper-resistant rice IR-36. But IR-36, while unpopular with planthoppers, fell an easy victim to a viral disease called tungro. As a result, the planthopper plague was quickly followed by an "explosion of the tungro virus":

The Explosion of the Tungro Virus

Tungro began to be a problem in Gianyar in 1980, and steadily increased until the explosion in 1983/84, destroying 421.15 hectares of rice completely, predominantly the variety IR 36 . . . A temporary remedy was found in the new rice variety PB 50. In one cropping season, tungro was reduced, but immediately afterward the new rice was afflicted by Helminthosporium Oryzae . . .

Following a, by now, familiar pattern, the new PB 50 rice proved vulnerable to two new diseases, as described in the Gianyar report:

The Explosion of Helminthosporium and Rice Blast

Problems with Helminthosporium Oryzae actually began in 1977/78 when five hectares were reported to be damaged. The explosion began in 1982/83 when 6007.95 hectares of paddy were afflicted . . .

Thus by the mid-1980s, Balinese farmers had become locked into a struggle to stay one step ahead of the next rice pest by planting the latest resistant variety of Green Revolution rice. Despite the cash profits from the new rice, many farmers were pressing for a return to irrigation scheduling by the water temples in order to bring down the pest populations. But to foreign consultants at the Bali Irrigation Project, the proposal to return control of irrigation to water temples was interpreted as religious conservatism and resistance to change. The answer to pests was pesticide, not the prayers of priests. Or as one frustrated American irrigation engineer said to me, "These people don't need a high priest, they need a hydrologist!"

STUDYING THE ECOLOGICAL ROLE OF WATER TEMPLES

In the spring of 1987, I began a new phase of research on the ecological role of the water temples in collaboration with a systems ecologist, Dr. James Kremer. My year of fieldwork in Bali (1983–84) had convinced me that the primary role of water temples was in the maintenance of social relationships between productive units. The question that Kremer and I wished to address was: did these systems of social coordination have measurable effects on rice production? The Green Revolution approach assumed that agriculture was a purely technical process, and that production would be optimized if everyone planted high-yielding varieties of rice as often as they could. In contrast, Balinese temple priests and farmers argued that the water temples were necessary to coordinate cropping patterns, so that there would be enough irrigation water for everyone, and pests could be reduced by coordinated fallow periods. Kremer suggested that these alternatives could be scientifically evaluated in an ecological simulation analysis. Furthermore, such an analysis might yield deeper insights into the reasons for regional differences in the organization of water temple networks.

Our first idea was to investigate cases in which water temples had been removed from irrigation management. But we quickly concluded that it would be impossible to learn very much from such a study, since it would be difficult to directly associate events such as pest infestations with the absence of temple control. Moreover, a temple-by-temple comparison would not reveal the effects of higher-level systems of coordination between temples. The water resources available to any single temple are affected to some degree by the irrigation schedules of their neighbors upstream, and we hoped to be able to evaluate the effects of such cooperative arrangements in water management. In order to evaluate the significance of this coordination, we decided to model all of the irrigation systems that lie between two rivers in south-central Bali, the Oos and the Petanu.

Based on my earlier fieldwork, we knew that water temples make decisions about cropping patterns by taking into consideration the trade-off between two constraints: water sharing and pest control. As previously noted, if everyone plants at the same time, they will also harvest at the same time, and a widespread fallow period can reduce pest populations by depriving them of food and/or habitat. On the other hand, if everyone plants the same rice variety at the same time to keep down the pests, then irrigation demand cannot be staggered and there will be water shortages. Striking an optimal balance between these two constraints is not a simple matter, since the choices made by upstream farmers have implications for their downstream neighbors, and constraints such as the amount of water available for irrigation vary by location and by season.

Consider a simple model consisting of two subaks, one upstream and one downstream. Assume that the water supply is constant but inadequate to meet the needs of

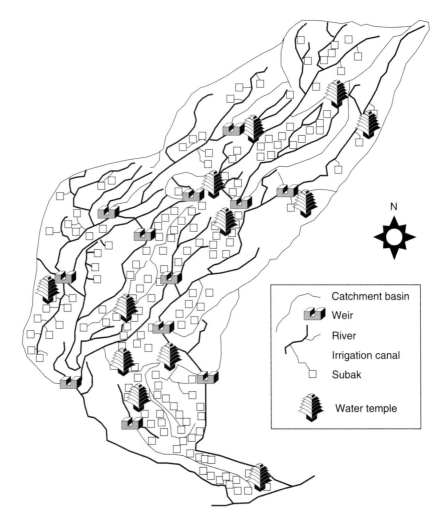

Figure 13   Computer model of irrigation along two Balinese rivers. This map (not to scale) shows the location of catchment basins, irrigation systems, and subaks along the Oos and Petanu rivers in south-central Bali.

both subaks at once, although sufficient if they stagger their planting schedules. Both subaks can suffer losses from the spread of rice pests.

Given these assumptions, we can immediately draw several conclusions: the upstream subak does not care about water scarcity, and so is free to choose any irrigation schedule. The downstream subak faces either water scarcity (under simultaneous cropping) or high pest damage (under staggered cropping) and will choose the lesser of two evils. If pest losses are high, both subaks will want to coordinate their planting schedule so that the pests will be reduced by a simultaneous fallow period. If pest losses are low, the upstream subak still wants to plant simultaneously to minimize pests, while the downstream subak prefers to stagger plantings so it will receive more water.

This simple model yields a basic insight into the logic of the temple system. If we paid no attention to the relationship between fallow periods and pest populations, it would seem that the upstream subaks would lack any incentive to cooperate with their downstream neighbors. But if we take the role of pests into account, we can see that upstream subaks have much to gain by cooperation. Helping their downstream neighbors satisfy their water needs is likely to be in their own self-interest, since it will allow them to synchronize irrigation schedules and reduce losses from pests. The model has the surprising result that under certain conditions, increasing the pests can lead to higher average rice yields![71]

The real world is a little more complicated: instead of two subaks, one upstream and one downstream, there are hundreds, and each one may influence ecological conditions for several neighbors. In order to gain an understanding of how these effects are transmitted, we built a computer model of all the subaks along two adjacent rivers in south central Bali. The purpose of the model was to evaluate the effects of social cooperation via temple networks on rice yields.

The watershed of the Oos and Petanu rivers includes approximately 6,136 hectares of rice terraces divided into 172 subaks. Based on topographical maps, we divided the watershed into 12 catchment basins and calculated the relationship between rainfall and stream flow for each of them. For each of the 172 subaks, we specified its location, area, the basin in which it is located, the dam from which it receives irrigation water, and the dam to which any excess water is returned. Given this geographical setting, the computer simulates the rainfall, river flow, irrigation demand, rice growth, and pest dynamics for all subaks on a month-by-month time scale. At the appropriate times, the harvest is adjusted for cumulative water stress and pest damage, yields are tallied, and the next crop cycle is begun.

The first use we made of this model was to compare the results of different types of social relations among subaks on harvest yields. It was possible to try multiple runs of the model, in which we kept all the biological variables the same but tried out different possible scales of social coordination:

- every subak is randomly assigned its own cropping pattern
- all the subaks follow the same cropping pattern
- half the subaks follow one pattern, and half plant a month later
- several other hypothetical patterns of coordination
- subaks plant in clusters based on the real patterns created by water temples

We were not really surprised to find that the last option (the water temple scale of coordination) produced the best harvests by finding the right balance between water sharing and pest control. But this result was important because it provided objective evidence that the water temples were playing a vital role in the ecology of the terraces.

But how well did our model reflect reality? To find out, I spent months working with a team of Balinese students to gather fresh data from our study area, so that we could test the harvests predicted by the model against real data. Figure 15 compares the model's predictions for each subak with real harvest data. There is a strong positive correlation. To make sure that these results were meaningful, we tried running the model with the same data (on crops planted, rainfall, etc.), but scrambled the

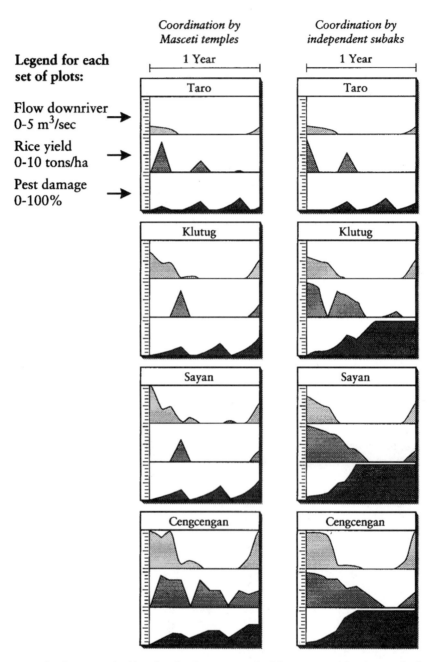

Figure 14   Comparison of yields with and without water temples. The computer model predicts simulated annual patterns for river flow, rice yield, and pest damage from the upper regions of the watershed (Taro) to the region nearest the sea (Cengcengan). Each of the three plots shows average results for the subaks in the area, over a twelve-month period (reading from left to right). The column on the left shows the effect of the coordination of planting schedules by large water temples (Masceti), while the column on the right shows the results of planting without temple coordination (in other words, each subak sets its own independent cropping pattern).

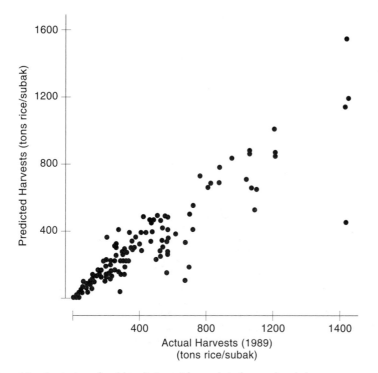

Figure 15   Comparison of model predictions with actual rice harvests by subak

planting dates. The correlation dropped to near zero, indicating that the synchroniza-
tion of cropping patterns by the water temples is highly significant for harvest yields.

WATER TEMPLES AS A COMPLEX ADAPTIVE SYSTEM

In 1993, a new insight into the workings of the water temple system appeared from
an unlikely source: complexity theory.[72] Imagine that the water temples don't exist,
but that all the known ecological changes along our two rivers are otherwise un-
changed. As a new year begins, each of our 172 subaks plants rice or vegetables. At
the end of the year, harvest yields are tallied. Now each subak checks to see whether
any of its nearest neighbors got a better total yield. If so, they copy the cropping pattern of their most successful neighbor. After all the subaks have decided to either
copy a neighbor or stick with their old cropping schedule, the computer simulates
another year of growth. The process continues until all the subaks decide to stick
with their current cropping pattern. What will happen?

I created this computer experiment because I wanted to see if I could figure out
how the water temple system might have developed. Did someone have to design it,
or could it come into existence spontaneously?

Figure 16 shows the distribution of cropping patterns for the first year in this experiment. Each symbol indicates a different cropping pattern; you can see that they

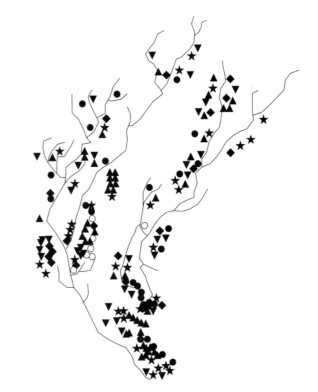

Figure 16   First run of a model of coadaptation. Each symbol indicates a different cropping pattern, randomly distributed among subaks in the Oos-Petanu watersheds. Average harvest was 4.9 tons of rice per hectare.

are pretty random. The average harvest for this run was 4.9 tons of rice per hectare. Figure 17 shows the pattern eight years later. See how the symbols have clustered in groups, representing local groups of subaks that are following the same schedule. The average harvest has almost doubled, to 8.57 tons. Now have a look at Figure 18, which shows the patterning created by the actual system of water temples. As you can see, the last two figures are nearly identical.

I was pretty excited when I ran this program for the first time and saw patterns that closely resembled water temple networks emerge out of randomness. Things got even more interesting as we ran more simulations, twiddling the dials on the physical and biological variables (rainfall, pest dispersal rates, etc.), and watched to see what happened. As long as we stayed within the bounds of biological possibility, the same phenomena occured: in less than forty years, a complex structure of coordinated cropping patterns emerged, which bore a remarkable similarity to the actual pattern of water temple coordination along these rivers. And as the artificial temple networks formed, harvest yields steadily increased.

Once these artificial water networks form in the computer, they display another interesting property: the ability to recover quickly from perturbations like low rainfall or a new kind of pest. Such disturbances appear as a cascade of changes that propagate through one or more clusters of subaks, but the temple network quickly adjusts. Yields remain higher than if the temple system were to stop functioning (as it did during the Green Revolution), leaving every subak to set its own individual cropping pattern.

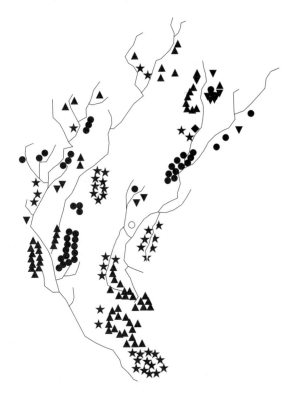

Figure 17   Last run of the model. Average harvest yields rose to 8.57 tons per hectare. Note the clusters of subaks following identical cropping patterns.

These results had several implications, both practical and theoretical. The main practical implication was that, in the computer, the emergence of temple networks leads to higher average yields and improvements in sustainability (the ability to cope well with changes in the environment). It appears that the temple networks are intrinsically capable of doing a better job of management than either uncoordinated planting (the Green Revolution system of "every man for himself") or centralized governmental control.

On a theoretical level, the computer model gives us a new way to think about the development of complex, sophisticated systems of irrigation management like the water temples of Bali. Our models show that the structure of water temple networks could have developed through a process of trial-and-error adaptation by the farmers, rather than deliberate planning by royal engineers or other planners. In the future, we hope to be able to compare test this idea against real archaeological data to see if the actual historical development of water temple networks follows the logic of coadaptation we see in the computer model.[73]

CONCLUSION: ARE THE WATER TEMPLES OBSOLETE?

Water temple networks are social creations, a social response to the problem of sustaining the rice terraces as productive ecosystems. The physical facts of interdependency in the irrigation systems and the need to create coordinated fallow periods for

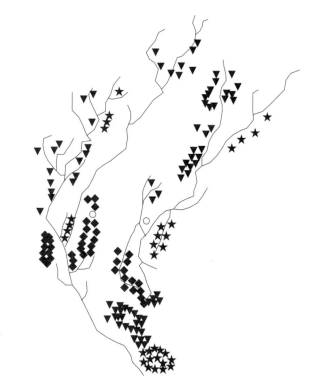

Figure 18   The distribution of cropping patterns in the traditional system of water temple networks. Note the similarity to Figure 17.

pest control place a premium on cooperation. All farmers who share water from the same source must cooperate in construction, maintenance, water allocation, and the management of disputes. Water temples link the physical features of irrigation systems to the social world of the subaks according to a logic of production: the congregation of a temple consists of the farmers who obtain water from the irrigation component "controlled" by the temple's god. Inside each temple, along with the shrine to the temple's principal deity, there are additional shrines for other gods. Offerings to these gods provide a way for the temple congregation to acknowledge their relationships to other temples and the social and physical units they represent. Finally, our ecological models suggest that the networks of relationships created in this way play a vital role in the ecology of the rice terraces.

But the practical importance of this traditional system of resource management was not apparent to development planners. At first, the very existence of the temple networks was not recognized. Later plans for irrigation projects by international development agencies foresaw an end to the productive role of water temples "as an almost inevitable result of technical progress."[74] For this reason, Kremer and I felt that it was important to bring the results of our analyses to the attention of development planners, who were not always eager to hear from us. Irrigation specialists from the Ford Foundation kept advising us (and our Balinese colleagues) to focus on individual farmers or subaks, and forget about modeling water temples. But as time went on, we began to receive a more sympathetic audience. The final evaluation report for the Bali Irrigation Project reversed the planner's earlier skepticism towards water temples:

The substitution of the "high technology and bureaucratic" solution in the event proved counter-productive, and was the major factor behind the yield and cropped areas declines experienced between 1982 and 1985. . . . The cost of the lack of appreciation of the merits of the traditional regime has been high. Project experience highlights the fact that the irrigated rice terraces of Bali form a complex artificial ecosystem which has been recognized locally over centuries.[75]

The report noted that erosion of the strength of the traditional vertical integration among water temples threatens "the long term sustainability of the irrigation systems."[76] It concluded with the observation that "no post-evaluated project of the Bank exhibits self-sustained and high performance comparable to Bali."[77]

But perhaps the most satisfying result was the visit of the Project Evaluation Mission to the Temple of the Crater Lake, described in the language of officialdom:

The Project Evaluation Mission interviewed leaders of the high Water User Group at Batur who have been instrumental in the proper establishment of some 45 new subaks during the last ten years. Apart from providing the required spiritual background, they often provided technical advice, for example on spring development, canal and tunnel siting and building, and clarifying water allocation issues. In light of the minimal success of the Project Office to develop new irrigation areas, it is suggested that there would be benefit from seeking advice from them. At the least, it is considered that this exercise would be of assistance in bringing the two parallel water development and management institutions into closer contact and could have more far-reaching impacts.[78]

At the time of this writing, official policy towards irrigation and water temples in Bali is in a state of flux. There is a continuing need to sustain high levels of rice production, and also to divert some flows formerly used for irrigation to urban uses. Nonetheless, for the first time, the water temples have achieved recognition by state irrigation bureaucracies, and for now the temples have regained informal control of cropping patterns in most of Bali.

NOTES

49. Geertz, *Negara*, 82.
50. *Statistical Yearbook of Bali 1986*, published by the Statistical Office of Bali Province, Jl. Raya Puputan Denpasar, Bali:8.
51. Rajapurana Ulun Danu Batur Vol. II:24 28.b.1, stenciled manuscript, library of the Bali Museum, Denpasar, Bali.
52. *Journal of a Tour along the Coast of Java and Bali & with a Short Account of the Island of Bali, Particularly of Bali Baliling*. Printed at the Mission Press of the Singapore Christian Union, Singapore, 1930, p. 24.
53. F.A. Liefrink, "Rice Cultivation in Northern Bali," in J.L. Swellengrebel, ed., *Bali: Further Studies in Life, Thought and Ritual* (The Hague, 1969).
54. Stukken ajkomstig van P.A.J. Moojen (architect, kunstschilder), "Kultuurprobleme," stukken voornamelijk betreffende de restauratie van tempels op Bali, met platte gronded. Ca. 1930. 1 bundel. H 1169:17, KITLV, Leiden. P. 21, letter to His Excellency the Governor General of the Nederlands-Indies, 21 January 1919.
55. "Memorie van Overgave der onderafdeeling Kloengkoeng," door Controleur J.C.C. Haar, 27 May 1926–3 Feb. 1930, pp. 22–24 (Leiden: Archives of the Koniinklijk Instituut voor Taal-, Land- en Volkenkunde).
56. The Balinese word that I have translated as "virgin priestess" is Jero Balian. There are two such priestesses at the temple, the elder (*duuran*) and younger (*alitan*). Each is herself chosen by a Jero Balian,

upon the death of her predecessor. Unlike the male priests of the temple, the virgin priestesses may not marry. They are the only priests of the temple who act as trance mediums (balian).

57. The Balinese term is *Pedanda siwa*. For a description of the role of Brahmana high priests in the preparation of holy water, see Christiaan Hooykaas, *Surya-Sevana: The Way to God of a Balinese Siva Priest* (Amsterdam: Verhandelingen K.N.A.W., nieuwe reeks, Deel 72/3, 1966).

58. A "weir" (*empelan*) is a diversionary dam in the river, which channels all or part of the flow into an irrigation canal. Almost always in Bali, this canal begins as a tunnel, since the rivers lie at the bottom of deep ravines.

59. Bali is divided for administrative purposes into eight administrative regions called kabupaten. At the head of each kabupaten is an official called the bupati, whose role with respect to his kabupaten is likened to that of the governor for the province of Bali. Each kabupaten is itself subdivided into half a dozen or so sub-districts called kecamatan. I have followed the usual practice of translating kabupaten as "regency."

60. Probably the Jero Gde meant that the flow from the spring amounted to about a hundred liters per minute, produced by the watershed area above the spring.

61. This is the typical pattern along the Oos and Petanu rivers, and more generally, in Bangli, Gianyar, and Badung. Elsewhere, there are other patterns of water temples that await investigation.

62. Roelof Goris, *Prasasti Bali I* (Bandung: N.V. Masa Baru, 1954), 55. The inscription is 002. Bebetin A1:IIb.4 (*undagi pangarung*).

63. Eugene Odum, *Basic Ecology* (New York: CBS College Publishing, 1983), 490–491.

64. Shoichi Yoshida, *Fundamentals of Rice Crop Science* (Manila: International Rice Research Institute, 1981), 147–151; Surajit K. DeDatta, *Principles and Practices of Rice Production* (New York: John Wiley & Sons, 1981), 297–298.

65. Laporan Statistik Pertanian ("Reports on Agricultural Statistics"), Dinas Pertanian Daerah Bali, Kantor Statistik Pulau Bali, Renon, Bali.

66. IRRI estimates an average growth of 105 days for IR-36, whereas the fastest-growing native Balinese varieties take about 135 days. However, as we will see, the rapid growth of high-yielding varieties of rice is not an unalloyed benefit, but a question of tradeoffs. Native Balinese rice takes longer to mature, and puts more of its energy into the whole plant rather than the seeds. Consequently, it is more resistant to disease and other stresses in its environment.

67. Anon., *Bali Irrigation Project Feasibility Study Part 2, Volume 5A (Subak Improvement Schemes)*. Manila: The Asian Development Bank, 1981. Consultant's report prepared by Electroconsult International, Milano, Italy, and Agricultural Development Corporation, Seoul, Korea, for the Directorate of Irrigation, Ministry of Public Works, Republic of Indonesia, January 1981.

68. Ibid., pp. 1–7.

69. *Bali Irrigation Project Feasibility Study Part 2, Volume 5A (Subak Improvement Schemes)*, pp. 1–2. The economic evaluation described in this study assumes that the project will generate $15,360,000 per year in increased rice production (pp. 1–8).

70. Project Performance Audit Report, Bali Irrigation Project in Indonesia. Asian Development Bank Post-Evaluation Office PE-241 L-352-INO (Manila, Philippines, May 1988), 47.

71. When crops are staggered, the aggregate yield falls due to pest damage to *both* fields, as opposed to simultaneous cropping in which there is water stress in only the downstream subak. But if the pest damage is low, the downstream subak may prefer staggered planting to minimize water stress. Higher pest levels provide an incentive to the downstream subak to prefer simultaneous cropping, even though this means somewhat higher losses from water stress. So there exists a theoretical range of pest levels such that increasing the amount of pest damage in the model can result in higher aggregate yields by compelling the downstream subak to switch to synchronized planting.

72. A good popular introduction to complexity theory is Roger Lewin's *Complexity: Life at the Edge of Chaos* (N.Y.: Macmillan, 1992). A general scientific introduction is provided by Stuart Kauffman, *The Origins of Order: Self-Organization and Selection in Evolution* (Oxford University Press, 1993).

73. See J.S. Lansing and J.N. Kremer, "Emergent Properties of Balinese Water Temple Networks: Coadaptation on a Rugged Fitness Landscape." *American Anthropologist* 95:1 (March 1993):97–114.

74. Project Performance Audit Report, Bali Irrigation Project in Indonesia. PE-241, L-352-INO, Restricted. May 1988: The Asian Development Bank, Manila, Philippines, 47.

75. Project Performance Audit Report, Bali Irrigation Project in Indonesia. PE-241, L-352-INO, Restricted. May 1988: The Asian Development Bank, Manila, Philippines, 48–50.

76. Ibid., 47.

77. Ibid., 50.

78. Ibid.

5 / Bali and the West

... it is the more painful that in the press voices were heard to attack this noble manifestation of honor, based on the bad government by the kings of Badoeng and also in view of the possibility that their readiness to die was only the workings of opium or arrack liquor.

—from an account of the 1906 Dutch war against the Balinese kings,
by H.M. van Weede (an eyewitness)

INTRODUCTION

Our subject in this concluding chapter is what anthropologists term *ethnohistory.* You may be excused for wondering whether there is a need for such a word: why not simply *history?* The anthropologist's answer is that history is generally written from the perspective of Western historians, whereas ethnohistory attempts to consider the views of members of non-Western societies. History is written by the victors, as someone said, and in their confrontations with Western powers, the Balinese were seldom victorious.

We'll begin with an account of two unusual Balinese poems. One was composed by a high priest who was apparently an eyewitness to the Dutch conquest of the Balinese kingdom of Badoeng. The war ended with a *puputan,* a word that means "ending" in Balinese, in which the king and his entire court were massacred in a suicidal attack on the Dutch army. This was not the first puputan in Balinese history; we know of other wars between Balinese kingdoms that ended in this way. But the puputan of the king of Badoeng was a more final ending, a moment of terror that the old priest saw as marking the end of his world. His story, the "Bhuwana Winasa" ("Annihilation of the Realm"), describes the events leading up to the war in Badoeng, and the beginnings of Dutch rule.

Recently a second poem was discovered in the loot from the burnt palaces of Badoeng. This poem, the "Purwa Senghara" ("Origin of the World's End"), was composed by the last king of Badoeng himself, less than a year before his death in the Dutch invasion. The "Purwa Senghara" is a long, elegant manuscript, written in a beautiful hand, that begins with the story of a hero's anguish as he sees a great kingdom about to be overrun by all-powerful but mindless demons:

Again Lord Arjuna asked the sage Bhagawan Abyasa
How can the kingdom of Dwarawati fall?
For it is justly ruled by Krishna
The god Wisnu himself watches over this land[79]

Arjuna's quest for an answer to the problem of the triumph of brutality over justice is the subject of this poem. The two poems together provide a comprehensive account of the Dutch invasion as seen by their Balinese foes. In the "Purwa Senghara" we see the real poet-king musing over the choices made by the gods and heroes of classical mythology as they faced impossible odds. Which is better, the calm resignation of Lord Buddha, or the heroic death of the warrior? The poem moves from kingdom to kingdom, examining how each one chose to meet its end.

While the kingdoms described in the "Purwa Senghara" belong to the mythical past of epic poetry, the real king of Badoeng faced the same dilemma less than a year after he finished the poem, when a fleet of Dutch warships appeared off his coast. He did not survive to write the history of the fall of his own kingdom, but the story of how he made his decision is told by the priest Ida Pedanda Ngurah of Mengwi in the "Bhuwana Winasa." This poem introduces us to the real, historical poet-king as he prepared to meet the Dutch invasion. The narrative describes the death of the king and his court, an event that is also described by those who would later write the "history" of the conquest of Badoeng: war correspondents from Dutch newspapers who accompanied the Dutch troops. The accounts by the Balinese priest and the Dutch journalists do not differ very much in their descriptions of the actual battle, but there is a world of difference in how they interpet its meaning.

Although the topic of this chapter is the encounter of the Balinese with the Western world, its real theme is the significance of the past for understanding the present. In recent years, as I have become more knowledgeable about Balinese culture, I find that I spend more and more of my time working with Balinese friends and colleagues to recover the meaning of events and stories like the history of the Temple of the Crater Lake, or the death of the king of Badoeng. The story of the king began for me one evening when I was visiting Ida Bagus, working on the translation of a text about agriculture. Quite unexpectedly a very well-dressed delegation of about twelve people arrived, members of the princely family of Badoeng. While the king and his immediate family had all died in the invasion, several cousins had survived, and it was their descendants who had come to see us. A member of the family had recently watched my film "The Three Worlds of Bali," which includes photographs of the war taken from the Dutch archives. A spokesman explained that these photographs were of great interest to the family, and asked for my help in acquiring copies. In return, they told me about the discovery of the "Purwa Senghara," the king's poem, which had deeply affected them. Before they knew about the poem, many Balinese had reluctantly accepted the view that the king had probably been drugged with opium or liquor, and that the puputan was a somewhat senseless act of defiance. The discovery of the "Purwa Senghara" allowed the king to tell his own story to his descendants.

LOST CAUSES AND IMPOSSIBLE ODDS (THE "PURWA SENGHARA")

To understand how the king of Badoeng saw the world in our year 1906 and his year Icaka 1827, we need to know something about prior Dutch relations with the Balinese.

At the beginning of the twentieth century, the military strength of the Dutch was no secret to the Balinese. The Dutch empire in the Indies had begun in the seventeenth century, and by the close of the nineteenth century most of this vast region—an archipelago stretching over an area roughly the size of the United States—was under Dutch control. The colonial empire was ruled from a city in Java called Batavia (modern Jakarta).

The nineteenth century was the age of Joseph Conrad's *Lord Jim* and *Almayer's Folly,* a period of more or less continuous armed struggles between the Dutch empire and what they referred to as the "native states" of the Indies. Bali was considered a valuable prize, and in 1846 the Dutch launched the largest military expedition they had yet dispatched against any of the "native states" to conquer the island, beginning with an attack on the kingdom of Buleleng on the north coast. The Balinese strongly resisted, and the Dutch eventually called off their attack. The failure of this expedition led to a second in 1848, and an even larger one in 1849.[80] The Third Expedition did succeed in conquering the kingdom of Buleleng, although at the cost of heavy casualties. But the invasion began to founder as the Dutch tried to complete their conquest of the island. Shortly after petitioning Batavia for reinforcements, the supreme commander of the Dutch forces was killed. When reinforcements finally arrived, the new commander declined to press the attack, and contented himself with a series of treaties with the remaining "sovereign kingdoms" of Bali: Klungkung, Gianyar, Bangli, Tabanan, Karangasem, and Djembrana. The key agreement was signed with the king of Klungkung, whom the Dutch recognized as the "Emperor" of Bali. In return for pledges not to enter into agreements with other "white men," to refrain from interference with Dutch shipping, to provide assistance to shipwrecks, and to allow Dutch representatives to remain permanently on the island, the Dutch promised not to "interfere with the governance of the Emperor":

> The Government of the Dutch Indies states that so long as the Emperor in the lands of Klungkung complies with the above agreements, the Government shall not in any way attempt to establish itself in this land or interfere with the governance of the Emperor.[81]

But despite these assurances, having established themselves in the north of the island, the Dutch searched for ways to extend their power over the southern kingdoms. A senior Dutch officer called a "controleur" was placed in charge of the governance of north Bali in 1855. For a few decades, while the Dutch made no further attempts at territorial conquests, strategies for completing the conquest of the island were the main topic of a secret administrative correspondence between the controleur of north Bali and his superiors in Batavia.[82] Most of these documents have been declassified by now, and are available to scholars in the colonial archives of the Netherlands. They indicate that in the 1880s a new phase of imperial expansion began with the creation of a high-level Dutch administrative unit called a "residency" for Bali and Lombok. Lombok is an island to the east of Bali, which was conquered by the east Balinese kingdom of Karangasem in the eighteenth century, and subsequently ruled by the Balinese princes of Karangasem. In 1894, the Dutch resident persuaded his superiors to embark on an invasion of Lombok.

As it was intended to do, the invasion of Lombok provided a dress rehearsal for the conquest of the kingdoms of south Bali. In November, a large Dutch force landed on the beaches of south Lombok. But the expedition met unexpectedly determined resistance and lost so many casualties that the army commander, General Vetter, sought permission to return to Batavia. Instead, he was sent reinforcements and ordered to attack. On November 18, 1894, he destroyed the main palace of Cakranegara, suffering 166 casualties among his own men and killing approximately two thousand Balinese. The palace strongrooms yielded a fortune in treasure: 230 kilograms of gold; 7,299 kilograms of silver; and three cases of jewels and ornaments, all of which were shipped back to Batavia.[83] The king survived the destruction of his palace, but was captured and died in exile six months later.[84]

With the fall of the Balinese princes of Lombok, the east Balinese kingdom of Karangasem also passed into Dutch control.[85] Soon two more of the southern Balinese kingdoms, Bangli and Gianyar, signed treaties by which they acquiesced to Dutch imperial sovereignty. But three of the Balinese kingdoms remained defiant: Badung, Tabanan, and Klungkung. In 1904, J.B. van Heutz became governor general of the Dutch East Indies. Van Heutz was a veteran of bloody military campaigns in Sumatra, a hard-liner who immediately launched a policy of conquest against the remaining independent "native states" of the Indies. Within a few months after taking office, van Heutz appointed a new resident for Bali and Lombok. In his memoirs, the new resident describes his first interview with van Heutz, who led him to a map of Bali and "running his hand across the principalities of South Bali said no more than 'this all has to be changed.' "[86]

In a matter of months, a military expedition was assembled to complete the conquest of Bali.[87] It seemed possible that a mere show of force would compel the surrender of the Balinese kings, who could not hope to prevail against a modern army. The official reason for the attack was the refusal of the king of Badoeng to pay com-

Dutch infantry before the gates of the palace

pensation for a shipwreck. The Dutch claimed that the villagers had looted the wreck. The villagers went to their temple and swore that the Dutch accusations were untrue, which was enough to convince their king.

Journalists from the major Dutch newspapers joined the expedition, as war correspondents, to record the inevitable triumph of a force that included three battalions of infantry, batteries of field artillery, and even a detachment of seven hundred cavalry. After the war, one of the war correspondents named H.M. van Weede wrote a book about his experiences. Here he describes the scene on the eve of the departure of the Dutch expeditionary force:

> That evening a ball was given at the marble hall and in the beautifully illuminated gardens of the Concordia Society. As always, this Concordia party was glorious, too; it ended in a "Confetti Battle" which took place after supper in the gardens. Meanwhile, in other halls festivities had been organized in honor of the under-officers and lesser ranks.
>
> On the eve before our departure the high dining hall of the Hotel Des Indes was filled with little and big tables, where good-bye dinners were given for those about to depart, while the music did its share to heighten the atmosphere.
>
> At about seven (A.M.) everything was aboard; plenty of ladies, official persons and friends came on board now to make their good-byes, and a last toast was offered to the success and happy return of the troops. Then off we went, accompanied by loud ovations from the audience on the pier . . .[88]

After a four-day sail from Surabaya, the Dutch warships carrying the expeditionary force positioned themselves off the southern coast of Bali. Over a period of days, the Dutch army embarked from their ships and advanced inland, fighting a series of skirmishes as they approached the walled palaces of Badoeng. Here is van Weede's eyewitness account of the invasion:

> The king was misled by our march on Sesetan, and convinced that we would try to approach from the south, he had placed all of his artillery there, and made everything ready for a concentrated defence. When he realized his error, it was too late to fortify the north and east sides of the capital. Besides, the increased artillery bombardment exercised a great loss of morale among his men. . . . Together with the old insane rajah of Pemacutan, to whose region the panic had spread, the king did not have more than 2000 men with weapons.
>
> Abandoned by most, the dishonor of exile before his eyes, and faithful to the customs of his religion, he then decided instead of surrenduring to have a *puputan,* that is, a general attack with lances, in which even women and children participate and in which all vow themselves to death . . .
>
> The king and the princes with their followers dressed in their most splendid clothes, and put on their krisses, whose golden hilts were in the shape of Buddha images and covered with gems; all were dressed in red or black and had their hair carefully combed and anointed with fragrant oil. The women had also put on their best dresses and jewels; most wore their hair loose and all wore white dresses. The king had someone set fire to the palace and destroyed anything inside it that could be broken. When he was informed at nine o'clock that the enemy had invaded Denpasar from the north, the tragic procession of 250 people started to move; every man and every woman carried a kris or long lance, children who were strong enough also carried weapons, and babies were carried in their arms. So they went to their destruction, north along the wide road planted with tall trees. The king went first, according to custom carried on the shoulders of one of his men, and

silently all together reached the crossing. . . . They went further until the dark line of our infantry became visible. That was the eleventh regiment, slowly pushing forward from the north. When they saw the resplendant procession, the Balinese were approximately 300 meters away; between the two groups there was a small plaza.

The troops were commanded to stop immediately and the interpreters were ordered by Captain Schutsel to order the approaching group to stop. This command was without result and in spite of repeated warnings, now the Balinese began to run. The captain and the interpreters continued to make signs, but in vain, and soon they had to accept the fact that they were dealing with people who were seeking death. Until a hundred—until eighty—until seventy paces, they were allowed to approach, but now they started to rush forward with their lances and krisses high in the air. To wait any longer would have been irresponsible for the safety of our men, and the first salvo was fired. One of the first to fall was the king, and now one of the most horrible spectacles one can imagine took place. While those who were saved continued the attack, and shooting fast remained necessary for our self-defense, one could see those who were wounded only slightly finish off the badly wounded. Women held up their chests to be finished off or got the coup de grace between the shoulders . . .

Van Weede describes how palace women threw pieces of gold at the soldiers and stood straight in front of them pointing at their hearts. The scene was one that even hardened colonial infantry could hardly stomach.

With the exception of a few that withdrew inside the houses, and of some wounded that later recovered, the entire heroic procession found the death they were seeking. A large heap of bodies lay in the middle of the small plaza where the encounter had taken place; the wives of the king bent over him, had let themselves be krissed, and many wounded had dragged themselves to him to cover him. His body was buried under their bodies, and out of this mass here and there gilded spear points protruded . . .

In a very somber mood the troops returned to their new bivouac in and around the palace; no one felt like mentioning anything about our unexpected and rapid success and thereby weakening the impression of the sorrow we had witnessed. The epic was over . . .[89]

But in fact the story was by no means over. A few weeks later, the Dutch army marched on Tabanan, a prosperous kingdom to the west. The king of Tabanan chose not to sacrifice his kingdom in a suicidal attack, and came to treat with the Dutch himself. But the Dutch took him prisoner and demanded an unconditional surrender. Van Weede was there:

Since I was standing behind the assistant resident, I had full opportunity to closely observe the Balinese dignitaries. I felt deep pity when a sadness bordering on despair appeared on their faces; still, at that moment they seemed to count a little on obtaining better conditions from the Comisaris of the government . . .

But at Denpasar the king learned that his wishes for immediate concessions were not considered possible, and that for the time being he would be sent into exile. . . . He spent the night in one of the pavilions of the palace. On the 29th, early in the morning, an escort arrived to take the prisoners: someone went to warn the king and his son, but when they entered the room, only their bodies were found. At the last moment, the king had cut the artery in his neck with a blunt sirih knife, and the young prince who such a short time ago still seemed to have a brilliant future before him, had become totally unrecognizable due to the effects of the poison he had taken.

THE KING'S POEM

When the bloody end of the kingdoms of Badoeng and Tabanan were reported in Dutch newspapers, there was speculation about the king's motives. As van Weede wrote, the prevailing view was that "the readiness to die they showed was only the result of the workings of opium or arrack liquour." But the poems written by the king and the high priest provide a very different context for the decision to carry out the puputan. Both poems are complex literary creations, with due attention paid to the rules of metrical construction we discussed in Chapter 3. There is obviously neither time nor space for full translations here, but by translating a few verses I will try to convey something of their essence.

Recall that the king's poem begins with Arjuna's question: how can a just kingdom be defeated? The sage Abhasa answers by explaining that nothing on earth can escape the endless cycles of life and death:

> You need not speak again of the sacred powers of Lord Wisnu
> Whose power to care for the realm and bring prosperity are without end
> Birth, life and death rule the world, even the gods cannot escape them.[90]

The sage explains that in the last phase of this cycle of the world, the powers of mindless destruction grow ever stronger until their ultimate triumph. This becomes the theme of the poem. The kingdom of Dwarawati is destroyed by thousands of rampaging demons, and a sorrowful Arjuna goes to the forest to meditate. Meanwhile, Wignotsawa, a demonic incarnation of the destroyer god Rudra, attacks the heaven of the divine nymphs, who cannot resist. The gods attempt to come to the rescue of the nymphs, but are vanquished by Wignotsawa's army of demons. On earth, the Buddha is reincarnated in the body of the greatest king of this age, Sutasoma, but the signs of immanent destruction continue, as Rudra reappears in the body of a gigantic flesh-eating demon. Sutasoma courageously offers his own body as food for the demon, but this is not enough to stop the dissolution of the kingdom. The poem ends with premonitions of a "horrifying war."

The poet-king draws several lessons from his catalogue of lost battles and unequal contests. The most important is the need to avoid having one's spirit "poisoned" by lingering too long on earth during the final age:

> Because the world has entered the final age
> The best are unwilling to remain in it for long.
> Their duties completed, they quickly depart this earth
> Aiming for the heavens.
> They fear to be corrupted by the poisons of the Age of Kali.[91]

Kali is the demonic female aspect of the destroyer god Siwa. In Balinese thought, she is incarnated in Rangda, the queen of witches, whom we've met in earlier chapters. Elsewhere in the poem, the king explains that it is impossible to fight her demonic armies without losing one's own virtue: not only are the demons far too numerous, but they attack in horrible ways and do not follow the rules of war. They cannot be beaten, and to fight them is to risk contamination by the poisons of the age of Kali. Better, then, for one's spirit to return quickly to heaven, and await the next age of the world.

THE PRIEST'S POEM

The poem of the priest Ida Pedanda Ngurah takes us from the realm of myth and legend to the actual events in Bali before and after the Dutch invasion. Yet the style of the poem and the events it describes are quite similar to those of the "Purwa Senghara."

> An envoy arrived, from the government of Java
> Called the Great Tuan,* a cunning man
> Accompanied by four others, all clever ones
> Arriving at the palace, all sat in chairs before the king.

> The Great Tuan spoke slowly, "My lord King,
> Will you pay for the goods from the shipwreck"?
> The King answered, "Why should this be my wish,
> I have not taken these things, nor my people at the seaside
> In brief, I shall not do so, for this is against our rights."

> The foreigners answered, "Our friend, this answer saddens us
> Perhaps our lord does not comprehend, this is a command
> Direct from the rulers of Batavia"†

The "Great Tuan," J. Eschbach, left immediately but sent an ultimatum to the king instructing him to pay the required compensation within two weeks or face a naval blockade. Meanwhile, the king began to meet with his counselors and also with the king of Tabanan, his neighbor to the west. The poem continues:

> The king of Badoeng spoke, "My lord princes,
> And my lord King of Tabanan, I am greatly pleased
> Even though disaster is coming, in your presence I feel
> The pure emotion in confronting whatever approaches
> Foretold in the Nitisastra‡ . . .
> As humans we cannot avoid our fate
> For all creatures life brings both happiness and sorrow."

Later, in a gathering of his ministers, the king spoke slowly: "Kinsmen and counselors, since it is certain that we will be conquered, what is your counsel? According to my belief, to choose the good according to our philosophy, we must fix the hour of our deaths. I therefore choose to seek Nirvana." The ministers agreed, saying, "Let us not be small-hearted, our wish is to perish in the battle, since your words are the truth, we shall become corpses." When the invasion began, the king hurried to complete the funeral rites for several kinsmen to fulfill his duties on earth. Meanwhile, the Dutch army advanced and was met by small groups of Balinese soldiers armed with lances, swords, and a few old firearms.

> Evening fell and the soldiers returned to their quarters
> But when the king arrived at his palace, he sought the high priest.
> "Om, om. Your servant asks the pardon of my lord priest,
> Tell me, what is the highest fate . . ."
> "Lord king, aim for sunia merta (perfect calmness)

---

* tuan: master
† Batavia: the Dutch imperial capital
‡ Nitisastra: a classical religious text

To purify your thoughts, by thinking of God
God will be present, goodness will dam up madness,
Strive to find clarity, focus your being." The king answered
"Yes, lord priest, that is what your servant truly desires."

On the day of the final battle, the king gave the order to destroy the palace as artillery shells were falling around him. As one hero after the next is killed in skirmishes with the Dutch, an elderly woman (possibly the king's mother) calls on her
beloved child to end her life with a sword stroke. Tears fall as she dies, and the procession goes out to meet the Dutch. The king appears calm and assumes the posture
of semadi meditation, before he is struck down by rifle fire. The court ladies, dressed
in their white cremation gowns

Marched forward like white ants,
But the bullets of their enemies were like fire
As they came forward and fell, their bodies piled up
A mountain of corpses in a sea of blood.

With the deaths of the kings and thirty-six hundred followers, the "world is washed
with blood." Looking back, the poet sees that there were signs foretelling the end:

Now the kingdoms have been defeated, fated by the All-Powerful,
There was a sign, the shrine of the king of Badung
At the Temple of Suaragiri was inundated by rains.
The shrine collapsed, and the place of the gods at Uluwatu
Likewise was destroyed by a thunderbolt.
The Hall of Audience at the palace of Pemetjutan,
Blown apart by the winds.
The beautiful beringan tree of Tabanan enveloped in spider's webs
So that it turned white, a sign of great danger.

The poem goes on to describe the first years of Dutch rule, marked by other
signs of disaster, including a devastating earthquake in 1917, in which more people
died and great temples were destroyed. Near the end of the poem, the priest describes his own life under the Dutch:

Frightened of death, I work on the road building
Breaking stones into fragments, sand for their roads.
Oppose the commands of the Tuan Controleur, and it is certain
The boat will come for me and I will be taken away.[92]

[Note: many Balinese rebels were sent into exile.]

OPIUM RECONSIDERED

With the fall of Badoeng and Tabanan, only the kingdom of Klungkung remained
undefeated. The story of the fall of Klungkung is bound up in a history that has only
recently come to light: the politics of opium. As W.F. Wertheim, a prominent Dutch
historian and former colonial civil servant, wrote in a foreword to a recent study of
opium in the Dutch colonies:

At the turn of the century, hardly had a colonial war ended before the first building would go up in the conquered territory—the office of the government opium monopoly![93]

But Wertheim also observed that "one almost has the impression that since the turn of the century, there has been a taboo of silence on the subject of the politics of opium in the Netherlands Indies . . ."[94] The story of the role of opium in the conquest is particularly interesting in light of the judgment of "history" that it was responsible for the "irrational" behavior of the king of Badoeng.

In the former kingdoms of north Bali ruled by the Dutch in the nineteenth century, the income from taxes on opium amounted to approximately two-thirds of total annual revenues, with taxes on rice accounting for most of the remainder.[95] Important as the opium revenues were, they were soon to play an even greater role in colonial policy. In 1894, the year the Dutch invaded Lombok, the colonial minister of finance suggested a new plan designed to greatly increase government revenues from opium throughout the empire. Formerly, opium was sold by private traders called "opium-pachters," and the government obtained revenues by taxing opium imports. The finance minister proposed that the colonial government put the opiumpachters out of business, and assume direct control over all aspects of the opium trade as a government monopoly. This "opiumregie" (government opium monopoly) was tried out in Madura in 1894, yielding revenues to the government of 17,500,000 guilders. In the following year, the opium monopoly was extended to all Dutch possessions. The profits were immense: by 1914, the opium monopoly had generated total revenues amounting to nearly half a billion guilders.[96]

It is clear from the internal correspondence of senior Dutch officials that in the first decade of the twentieth century, extending the opium monopoly to each of the newly-conquered Balinese kingdoms, and ultimately to the whole island, was a principal goal of the colonial government. Opium was already traded in Bali, but it was not yet under Dutch control. In a secret report to the governor general written from his residency in Singaraja (north Bali) on December 26, 1907, De Bruyn Kops wrote:

> I think it is legitimate to use force if necessary—and be assured that only in the most necessary case will weapons be used—to persist with the installation of the opium monopoly on the island of Bali . . .[97]

The complete plan for Bali, drawn up by the chief inspector for the opium monopoly in Batavia and forwarded to the governor general on January 13, 1908, called for the sale of government opium over the whole of Bali. Packaged opium would be supplied from a central depot in Singaraja to 124 salesmen, under the supervision of 5 assistant collectors. Altogether, 127 permanent "points of sale" were to be established for the sale of opium in Balinese villages.[98]

The government attempted to impose the opium monopoly on Bali in the spring of 1908. As far as the major newspapers in Batavia were concerned, it was Balinese resistance to this plan that prompted the massacre of the court of Klungkung. Klungkung fell on April 28. A week later, as the first reports began to filter back, the *Bataviaasch Nieuwsblad* reported:

> At the establishing of the opium monopoly, troops were sent without warning (into Klungkung) to look for clandestine opium. It was the advent of these troops which made

the population go for its arms. This information seems in accord with the passage in our report from yesterday, which says that it is not so much the king himself who wants war as the population. . . . The role of the opium monopoly in this rebellion becomes even clearer when one learns that after the departure of our officer van Schauroth from Klungkung to the coast, all of the salesmen of the opium selling points were murdered.[99]

The king of Klungkung chose to follow the example of the king of Badoeng, and led his followers directly into the gunfire of the Dutch, while his palace was blown to rubble. The opium monopoly was quickly established, and, in the remainder of 1908, the colonial government obtained revenues of 273,000 guilders from Bali. Soon afterwards, as the opium monopoly took root in Bali, the profits to the government became enormous. In 1911, the Dutch sold 3.5 million guilders' worth of opium in Bali and Lombok.[100] It appears, then, that opium did play an important role in the downfall of the Balinese kings—but not quite in the way Western "history" would have it.

COLONIAL BALI

On May 4, 1908, when the first reports of the fall of Klungkung began to come in, a leading newspaper in Batavia editorialized:

> It seems clear to us that the government will switch over to direct government of the whole of Bali . . .[101]

Yet the type of government the Dutch established in Bali seems at first surprising, almost inexplicable. Although they conquered the island in the name of progress, they wholeheartedly embraced Balinese "feudalism." Rather than abolishing the Balinese kingdoms, the Dutch tried to strengthen them. Docile princes were placed in nominal control of each of the conquered territories, and colonial scholar-administrators studied the administrative workings of Balinese kingdoms as a model for colonial rule. Villagers were required to pay monetary taxes and also a "labor tax," working on projects such as the road building described in the "Bhuana Winasa." But these taxes and regulations were interpreted as a continuation of the traditional way of life in Balinese kingdoms. The Dutch even created new laws in support of the caste system: aristocrats were exempted from the labor tax, so they would not have to soil their hands with manual labor. This policy was passionately resented by many Balinese "commoners," and made caste a divisive political issue. Meanwhile, the Dutch went to some trouble to portray the real kings they had just defeated as decadent, corrupt despots. But if the Balinese aristocracy was so corrupt, why go to such lengths to support their "feudal" prerogatives?

Once again, I suggest that the answer lies not in Balinese culture, but in the culture of the colonial civil service, a deeply conservative institution. For a leading Dutch scholar-administrator, V. E. Korn, the "great failing" of the Balinese form of government was "the lack of a powerful government over the whole realm." Aristocratic Dutch colonial officers saw themselves as restoring kingdoms and institutions that the decadent kings of recent times had sadly neglected. As the possibility of revolt by real Balinese kings diminished, the civil service sought to strengthen the status and powers of their puppet princes. This policy finally culminated in a ceremony held at the supreme temple of Besakih in 1938, when both Dutch and Balinese rulers of Bali gathered for a grand ceremony of kingship. Eight Balinese aristocrats, draped with Dutch medals and Balinese gold, were consecrated as rulers (*Zelfbestuurders*) of the territories that the Dutch recognized as the eight former kingdoms of precolonial Bali. Balinese kingship, which had been obliterated by gunfire a generation earlier, was thus reconstituted in a ceremony that mingled the ritual paraphernalia of Balinese kingship and high colonial office. The cosmological significance of this ritual for the colonial administrators who organized it was signaled by their choice of time and place. Nineteenth-century Balinese kings were not consecrated at Besakih, or in any temple, but in their own palaces. But the Balinese believe that on the feast of Galungan, the supreme gods and the deified spirits of ancient kings descend to the temple of Besakih. By holding the ceremony at Besakih, the colonial civil service was inviting the spirits that had guided Bali in the past to witness the restoration of an enlightened monarchy. The colonial image of Balinese kingship would finally become tangible reality in the persons of these cultivated Dutch-speaking aristocrats, who would gently guide Bali into the modern age, under the wise tutelage of their personal Controleurs. In a letter written in 1940 to Korn, who had recently retired, Assistant Resident Cox wrote with satisfaction that

> Young Bali develops very well, but fortunately Old Bali has things still under firm control.[102]

For Cox, it seems, "Old Bali" had come to mean Dutch officers like himself as well as the princes. But the colonial vision of the future was soon to prove a mirage. On the 16th of February, 1942, the Imperial Japanese air force bombed the airport in Bali, and when the Japanese troops began to land the next day, they found the island undefended: the small detachment of colonial troops had fled to Java.

THE POST-COLONIAL ERA

At the beginning of this century, the population of Bali was less than a million; it will probably exceed 3 million by the end of the century. The Dutch built roads and irrigation dams, but otherwise did little to provide their Balinese subjects with education, public health, or economic opportunities. However, their laissez-faire policies of "peace and order" (*rust en orde*) are generally credited with creating the conditions for a kind of renaissance in the arts and religion in the 1920s and 1930s.

The defeat of the Japanese at the end of World War II was followed by a bloody struggle for independence. Indonesian nationalists who had fought a guerrilla war against the Japanese proclaimed the birth of the independent nation of Indonesia on August 17, 1945. But the Dutch decided to try to regain control of their former colonies, and Dutch forces landed on Bali in 1946. Most of the major events in the struggle for independence took place on the neighboring island of Java, but guerrilla warfare against the Dutch continued on Bali. When independence finally came in 1949, the new government of Indonesia was faced with economic disaster: it inherited the fragments of a colonial-plantation economy that was even further damaged by

years of war. The 1950s were a period of economic stagnation, inflation, rapid population growth, and growing poverty. Political parties fought savage battles for power,
which culminated in 1965 with the massacre of the Indonesian Communist Party
(PKI). Tens of thousands of ordinary Balinese labeled PKI were slaughtered by death
squads of other political parties, with the tacit approval of the armed forces. One of
the issues that caused the most bitter conflicts was the question of special privileges
for persons of high caste, which had been written into law in the colonial era.

The military government that came into power at the end of the massacres of
1965 had two immediate goals for Indonesia: political stability and an end to economic decline. Comprehensive five-year plans for economic development were
drawn up by senior government officials, some with doctorates in economics from
American universities. When the planners looked to Bali, attention focused on the
opportunities for growth in the tourist industry.

Tourism was already an old story in Bali. As early as 1914, the Dutch steamship
line had begun to advertise trips to Bali:

Bali

You leave this island with a sigh of regret and as long as you live you can never forget
this Garden of Eden.[103]

Tourists arrived on Dutch boats at a rate of about one hundred per month by the
1930s, drawn by an array of exotic images: "the island of bare-breasted women," "the
island of the gods," "the island of temples and dances." But tourism had fallen off
during World War II, and never recovered. In the 1960s, the nationalist government
took the first step toward a revival of the tourist industry by spending Japanese war
reparations to build a luxury hotel on the beach at Sanur. Ironically, this hotel (the
Bali Beach) stands at the very site where the Dutch invasion force landed in 1906!

In 1971, the World Bank created a master plan for economic development in
Bali, based on a planned expansion of the tourist industry. International hotel chains
were invited to go into partnership with investors (usually not Balinese), while the
government would subsidize enlargement of the airport. As the era of jumbo jets
began, a few Balinese who owned land in the areas slated for tourist development
became wealthy, but for most Balinese tourism meant jobs in what economists term
the "service sector," as hotel or restaurant workers.

Since the tourist industry continued to market Bali as an exotic "island of the
gods/dancers/bare-breasted women," the old Dutch roads soon filled with buses,
taxis, and cars ferrying visitors to see exotic spectacles. The need for such spectacles
provided an economic windfall for villages located along the roads leading from
the beach resorts up to the volcanoes. These villages soon began to market their
dances, rituals, woodcarvings, paintings, jewelry, or nearby archaeological sites to
the tourists. But the desire of these visitors to experience the "authentic" culture
promised in their guidebooks also led many of them to show up uninvited at religious rituals and insist on their right to be there as "adventurous" travelers.

Recently, many anthropologists working in Bali have turned their attention to
tourism, and its effects, as a social phenomenon worthy of serious study. Philip McKean
was working on this subject when I first met him in Bali in 1971. McKean learned that
tourism can play a constructive role by providing new sources of patronage for the

traditional arts. He studied the revival of an orchestra and dance troupe made possible by income from tourist performances. These musicians and dancers were able to perform for traditional religious occasions as well as for the tourists. I found a similar pattern with woodcarvers: young men from poor families in Sukawati studied wood-carving as a way to earn a living by creating objects for the tourist trade. Eventually, they were able to put their skills to use in the refurbishing of temples and traditional architecture.[104]

But my study and McKean's were done in the 1970s, when the number of tourists was a fraction of current levels. More recent studies have traced the effects of a kind of cultural schizophrenia created by the tourist industry: to fulfill the visitor's expectations, Balinese must act out the roles that have been created for them by endless advertising campaigns.[105] Balinese who are willing to work in the tourist industry are generally attracted by at least some aspects of the modern Western lifestyle displayed by wealthy tourists. But to fulfill the guidebook image of Balinese, they must disguise this attraction and play the role of exotic native. Desk clerks, hotel maids, and wood-carvers soon learn to enact the fantasy image for tourist after tourist. Over time, as whole villages are reorganized to attract tourist income, which is increasingly spent on Western consumer goods, the Balinese find themselves troubled with the post-modern dilemma of authenticity. In 1992, an article in the Indonesian language *Bali Post* attracted much attention with the provocative title "Are we still 'Balinese'?" Still, the growth of the tourist industry has provided employment for many Balinese in an era when population growth has rapidly increased. In 1979, the population of Bali was about 2,400,000. How many Balinese can continue to live a traditional lifestyle as farmers and villagers? In 1987 the planning board of the Balinese provincial government asked themselves this question. The answer they arrived at was about 2.5 million people. But by the time they had performed this calculation, the island's population had already exceeded 2,700,000.[106]

What does the future hold for the Balinese? There is quite a lot of good news. First, population. Not long ago, the picture looked quite bleak: the fertility rate for Balinese women in 1967–70 was 5.8 percent, which would have led to very rapid population growth. At that time, most demographers (population experts) held out little hope for societies like Bali: it was thought that fertility would only come down after a long period of economic growth and social change. Demographers assumed that "traditional" societies like Bali would resist family planning because of the importance of children for peasant households. But in the early 1970s a team of Balinese public health workers launched a new program designed to take advantage of one of the strongest pillars of Bali's "traditional" culture: the banjar system. Family planning workers made appointments to attend the monthly banjar meetings, in order to explain the advantages of smaller families. They could easily show that there was already a shortage of good farm land, a problem that would only intensify if everyone kept trying to have large families. After debating the issue, many banjars agreed that two children per couple was a worthwhile goal, and began to monitor the fertility and contraceptive use of their own members. By 1985, more than four thousand banjars had joined the "Banjar Family Planning Project," and the overall fertility rate for Bali had dropped to 2.6 percent. The success of the family planning project in Bali drew worldwide attention, and has led some demographers to rethink their strategies for controlling population growth, since it was precisely the strength of Balinese traditional society that made this program so successful.[107]

There is more good news with respect to family incomes and life expectancy. In 1979, government statistics estimated the per capita income of Balinese at 147,000 Indonesian rupiah. By 1985 this figure had more than tripled, to 550,495 rupiahs. One American dollar was worth about 1,100 rupiah in 1985, so this was equivalent to about $500. It should be noted, however, that these estimates are not very precise, and, more importantly, that the growth in income was far from uniform: most of the new wealth came from the expansion of the tourist industry. Tourist development was largely concentrated in the urban areas, and this difference in income levels shows up in life expectancy, which is presently 64.6 years for urban Balinese, and only 61.1 years for people living in rural areas.[108]

Looking to the future, government planners hope to see a continuation of the trends we've just considered: rising incomes, slower population growth, and continued expansion of tourism. But how many tourists can Bali hold? Current plans for tourist development anticipate 1.5 million tourists a year by the year 2000, by which time there will be about 3 million Balinese.[109] This means one tourist for every two Balinese, a sobering prospect for all but the most ardent promoters of the tourist industry.

> Reverse the spell, he cries,
> And let it fairly now suffice,
> The gambol has been shown.
> —Parnell's *Tale*

WORLD RENEWAL

The cosmic maps that Ida Bagus began to explain to me during my first fieldwork proved a trusty guide, and they will see us through to the conclusion of our final story: the great rituals of world renewal the Balinese have carried out in recent years to cope with the transformations set in motion by their encounters with the West.

The first of these rituals was held in 1963, during the period when the Balinese were experiencing great economic hardship and political turmoil. In the face of an apparently endless series of wars and disasters, a decision was made by Balinese religious leaders to hold an enormous ceremony of world renewal at the supreme temple of Besakih. Various lontar manuscripts stated that the end of a century was a major event that should be marked by a ceremony called Eka Dasa Rudra (Eleven Rudras). Rudra is the most powerful demon of destruction described in the "Purwa Senghara." Various sacred texts describe Rudra as an ancient Sanskrit destroyer god, the fierce demonic incarnation of the supreme god Siwa. The culmination of the Eka Dasa Rudra ceremony is an attempt to transform Rudra from an agent of chaos into his godlike form as Siwa.

In 1963, the end of the Icaka century was still seventeen years in the future. But the president of Indonesia, Sukarno, urged the Balinese priests to carry out the ceremony ahead of schedule, perhaps to mark a new beginning for his own regime. Sukarno invited a world congress of travel agents to attend, and preparations began at Besakih temple. A cosmic map was laid out just outside the temple gates, with

Crowds approach Besakih temple for the ceremony of world renewal.

shrines at each of the eight wind-directions and three more representing the zenith, nadir, and center of the universe. On the full moon of the tenth month, marking the beginning of the new year, blood sacrifices would be made at each of these eleven shrines, representing the demonic elements of Rudra in both the outer world of Bali (and the cosmos) and the inner world of the self. Afterwards, teams of high priests would pray for the transformation of Rudra into Siwa as the new year began.

Besakih temple is located high on the slopes of Bali's largest volcano, Mount Agung. As preparations for Eka Dasa Rudra began in February, Agung began to emit smoke and ash. While preparations continued, so did the signs of an imminent eruption. Ceremonies began on March 8, but four days later the eruption began in earnest, as red-hot rocks and ash rained down around the temple. By March 17, rivers of molten lava were flowing down the slopes, while smoke and volcanic ash blotted out the sun. An unknown number of Balinese died of asphyxiation, burns, and, later, starvation in remote villages cut off by rivers of lava.

The disastrous Eka Dasa Rudra of 1963 was followed by the massacre of thousands of alleged communists in 1965. The advent of mass tourism around 1970 helped improve Bali's economic fortunes, but in more subtle ways the rapid importation of Western culture posed yet another challenge to traditional Balinese culture. So when the true end of the Icaka century loomed in 1979, there was enormous interest in whether, this time, the Eka Dasa Rudra ceremony would have a better result.

The anthropological filmmaker Ira Abrams and I made a documentary film about the 1979 Eka Dasa Rudra ritual, which we interpreted as an enormous effort by the Balinese to try to impose their cosmological vision on the shape of events. I saw many parallels between this grand ceremony of world renewal and the ordinary

A Baris dancer welcomes the gods at Besakih temple.

rites of passage in a human life that we discussed in Chapter 2. Both ceremonies utilize a cosmic map, although rites of passage refer to the inner world of the self, while the rituals of world renewal focus on both the inner and outer worlds. But the imagery of the cosmic map is not the only similarity between these rituals. The structure of the ritual process is also broadly similar. Three levels of comparison occurred to me:

- an emphasis on the idea of cyclical patterns of change or transformation (*metemahan*) as a never-ending process in the inner and outer worlds
- the belief that death or dissolution can be followed by rebirth, in a dangerous time of passage

- the idea that the key to a successful transformation or passage is to bring the dangerous elemental powers (buta) under disciplined control

While filming the preparations for the ceremony in 1979, we recorded a broadcast from Bali's new television station by a religious leader, explaining the meaning of the ceremony in the new medium of television. His explanation picks up some of the same themes I have suggested. Here is what he said:

> To those honored persons who are about to watch this broadcast, peace and blessings to you. Now I wish to provide an explanation for you now hearing my words, of the ceremony we have under way, Eka Dasa Rudra.
>
> My explanation is based on the information provided by learned persons and also on the knowledge contained in sacred lontar manuscripts. The manuscripts which we have consulted included *Sundari Gamo, Asta Kosala Bumi,* and many others.
>
> Each year at the time of the Ninth Dark Moon, when the new Icaka year approaches, it is appropriate to make *tawur* sacrifices to the elemental powers. The tawur are given to the gods of the underworld, but they are accepted by the supreme deity so that the whole world can be cleansed and the welfare of the world's people sustained. It is necessary to hold this type of ceremony once each year.
>
> At the close of each cycle of five years, because the interval is longer, the ceremony is raised to a higher level of completeness. This is called Panca Wali Krama. At the close of a ten-year cycle, an even higher level ceremony is performed. And at the close of ten ten-year cycles, we must carry out the greatest of tawur sacrifices, called Eka Dasa Rudra. Now let me pose a question: why must we hold this ceremony after ten ten-year cycles?
>
> Followers of the Dharma, this is the explanation that is given to us by the learned. Every process of transformation, whether in the microcosm of the self, or the macrocos-

The author filming a Topeng performance at Besakih temple.

mos, always brings changes. Growing from a child to an adult brings change. Education from lower school to university brings many changes in one's experience and understanding. But change must happen in the right sequence, or it is dangerous. The need to keep change under control is the reason this ceremony must take place. Uncontrolled change can destroy peace, like the fire of Agni (the fire god), which is dangerous only when it is out of control.

These, in brief, are the motivations for the ceremony we are about to perform—Eka Dasa Rudra. This completes my task of explanation for television. Om, Santi, Santi, Santi.

At the instant the twentieth Icaka century began (March 28, 1979, at high noon on our calendar), eleven teams of high priests chanted their prayers towards the eleven-pointed cosmic map outside the gates of Besakih temple, while an audience consisting of visiting dignitaries and tens of thousands of Balinese patiently watched. At the center of the sacred enclosure were two small diagrams. One showed the god Siwa springing out of the demon Kala (who ravaged the world in the "Purwa Senghara"); the other, the mother goddess Uma emerging from Durga, the mother of witches. As the sun passed its zenith and the new century began, teams of temple priests emerged from the cosmic map with holy water and sprinkled it on the land and people.

NOTES

79. "Geguritan Purwa Senghara," Pupuh VIII/Pucung, verse 17, manuscript library of the Fakultas Sastra, Udayana University (my translation).

80. See J. van Swieten, *Krijgsbedrijven tegen het eiland Bali in 1848* (Amsterdam: Doorman, 1849); A.W.P. Weitzel, *De derde militaire expeditie naar het eiland Bali in 1849* (Gorinchem: Noorduyn, 1859); J.O.H. Arntzenius, *De derde Balisches expeditie in herinnering gebracht* (Den Haag: Belinfante, 1874); G. Nypels, *De Expeditie naar Bali in 1846, 1848 en 1849* (Haarlem: Vandorp, 1897).

81. E. Utrecht, *Sedjarah Hukum Internasional di Bali dan Lombok* (Bandung: Penerbitan Sumur Bandung, 1962), 340. The passage quoted is a translation of Article 15 of an agreement between the kingdom of Klungkung and the Dutch government, dated July 13, 1849.

82. For an overview of Balinese-Dutch relationships of this era, see Alfons van der Kraan, *Lombok: Conquest, Colonization and Underdevelopment 1870–1940* (Singapore: Heinemann, 1980). The correspondence between the controleurs of North Bali and Batavia is preserved in the Algemeene Rijksarchief in the Hague. See especially M.v.K. 1850–1900, Inventaris 6059, 31 December 1874 (Geheim); M.v.K. 1850–1900, Inventaris 6448, Mailr. 1885; M.v.K. 1850–1900, Inventaris 6496, Mailr. 1892 Nr. 872; Mailr. 1 July 1902, Mailr. no. 546.

83. Alfons van der Kraan, *Lombok*, 97.

84. Ibid., 99.

85. The Dutch were highly satisfied with their conquest, as is evident in a contemporary report: "In the meeting of the Governing Council of the Indies of the 30th of December 1904, Mr. Liefrinck, a member of the Council of India, showed that the Dutch government, after the war at Lombok, had no better subjects than the Balinese who lived on Lombok. From their side, no inimical attacks were made on us, and with the organisation of the argriculture as well as with the introduction of the new tax system, they provided us with a cooperation which increased our opinion of the value of their enlightened judgment." H.M. van Weede, *Indische Reisherinneringen* (Haarlem, H.D. Tjeenk Willink & Zoon, 1908), 413.

86. G.F. de Bruyn Kops, "Het evolutie tijdperk op Bali 1906–1915," in *Kolonial Tijdschrift 4* (1915):466

87. Algemeene Rijksarchief, Kol. na 1900, Inventaris 77, 12 October 1906 (Geheim/"Secret").

88. H.M. van Weede, *Indische Reisherinneringen* (Haarlem, H.D. Tjeenk Willink & Zoon, 1908), 408–410.

89. H.M. van Weede, *Indische Reisherinneringen* (Haarlem, H.D. Tjeenk Willink & Zoon, 1908), 462–477.

90. Jati tuhu paragan Sang Hyang Wisnu, tan nyandang parnayang
wireh pakumpulan lewih, Sang Hyang Wisnu, prasida sarining jagat.
Ne tetelu utpeti, stiti, puniki, tekaning pralina, kawisesa makasami,
twara nyandang, cening rahat manyakitang.
—"Purwa Senghara," Pupuh VIII, verse 19.

91. "Purwa Senghara," Pupuh XXXIII, verses 46–47.

92. "Bhuwana Winasa," original manuscript in the library of the Gedong Kirtya, Singaraja, Bali.
Pupuh VIII (Sinom), verses 6–7.

93. Wertheim adds, ". . . And was the expansion of the opiumregie perhaps not only a result that followed, but also one of the background motives for the expansion of power?" (my translation). W.F.
Wertheim, Voorwoord to Ewald Vanvugt, *Wettig Opium* (Haarlem: Knipscheer, 1985), 11.

94. W.F. Wertheim, Foreword to Ewald Vanvugt, *Wettig Opium* (Haarlem: Knipscheer, 1985), 10.
Wertheim adds: ". . . I researched the well-known handbooks of Netherlands Indies history, and had to
conclude that in most of them the opium politics of the government are only mentioned casually. The
same goes for the well-known handbooks of economics. You can find something there about the opium
monoploy of the VOC and about the Chinese opiumpachters of the nineteenth century—but it is as if with
the suspension of the opiumpacht and the introduction of the opiumregie, around the turn of the century,
the question lost its interest."

95. H. van Kol, *Uit onze Kolonien* (Leiden: A.W. Sijthoff), 519: "In vroeger jaren bedroeg de invoer
van opium bijna twee derde van den totalen invoer a 3,400,000 gulden." See also ARA Mailr. 1 July 1902,
Mailr. no. 546, "Vergelijkend overzicht van de Uitkomsten der opiumverpachtingen in eenige geweesten
ter Bezittingen buiten Java en Madoera over de jaren 1901 en 1902," which reports total income from
opium sales in Bali as fl. 102,240 in 1901 and fl. 108,060 in 1902.

96. In the years 1904, 1906, 1908, and 1911 the opium monopoly yielded respectively fl. 14,523,000;
fl. 15,177,000; fl. 14,741,000, and fl. 16, 375,000. H. van Kol, *Weg met het Opium!* (Rotterdam: Masereeuw
& Bouten, 1912), 18. In 1912, the Colonial Yearbook reports that a total of 1,599,928 thails of opium of an
average purity of 41 percent yielded an income of fl. 23,262,000. Bijl. A.A. of the *Kolonial Verslag 1912.*

97. Secret letter to His Excellency the Governor General of the Netherlands Indies from W.G. de
Bruyn Kops, Resident of Bali and Lombok. Singaraja, 26 December 1907. Algemeene Rijksarchief, Den
Haag.

98. The administrative cost of the opium monopoly on Bali to the government was estimated by the
resident at fl. 32,280 per annum.

99. *Bataviaasch Nieuwsblad,* May 4, 1908. See also the articles in the colonial newspaper *De Loco-
motief* beginning April 30, 1908.

100. Total opium revenues from the Netherlands Indies in 1911 were fl. 23,262,000 from the sale of
1,599,928 thail (one thail = 38.6 grams). H. van Kol, *Weg met het Opium!* (Rotterdam: Masereeuw &
Bouten, 1913), 13–16. Ten years later, the sale of opium in Bali alone was worth over a million guilders a
year to the Dutch government. See the annual report of the opium controleur to the resident of Bali, dated
31 January 1923; as well as report 435 (197) of the Korn Collection, Koninklijk Instituut voor Taal-,
Land- en Volkenkunde (Leiden). The sale of opium was a steady source of income. In 1921, for example,
income from opium in Bali was fl. 1,127,377.

101. Bataviaasch Nieuwsblad, May 4, 1908. The Hague: Algemeene Rijksarchief (hereinafter
ARA).

102. Korn Collection in the Koninklijk Instituut voor Taal-, Land- en Volkenkunde, Leiden. Docu-
ment 138.

103. KPM tourist advertisement, reproduced in Wim Bakker, Bali Verbeeld, Delft: Volkenkundige
Museum Nusantara, 1985:30.

104. Lansing, "Economic Growth and the Traditional Society: A Cautionary Tale from Bali,"
Human Organization 37(4): 391–394.

105. Recent studies of tourism in Bali include Adrian Vickers, *Bali: A Paradise Created* (Singapore
and Berkeley: Periplus Editions, 1989); Michel Picard, *'Tourism Culturel' et 'Culture Touristique,' Rite et
Divertissement dans les Arts du Spectacle á Bali,* these de doctorat de 3eme cycle, EHESS, Paris 1984;
and W. Donald McTaggart, "Some Development Problems in Bali," *Contemporary Southeast Asia* 6,
3(1984):152–169.

106. *Rencana Pembangunan Lima Tahun Propinsi Daerah Tingkat I Bali (Repelita V Daerah),*
1989/90–1993/94:8. Denpasar: Government of Indonesia.

107. *Monografi Program Keluarga Berencana Nasional Propinsi Bali.* Denpasar, Bali: Badan Ko-
ordinasi Keluarga Berencana Nasional, Renon:68–70.

108. Ibid., 42, 62.

109. *Manfaat Pariwisada Dalam Menunjang Pembangunan Daerah Bali.* Denpasar, Bali: Pemerin-
tah Propinsi Tingkat I Bali, 1991:22.

Appendix

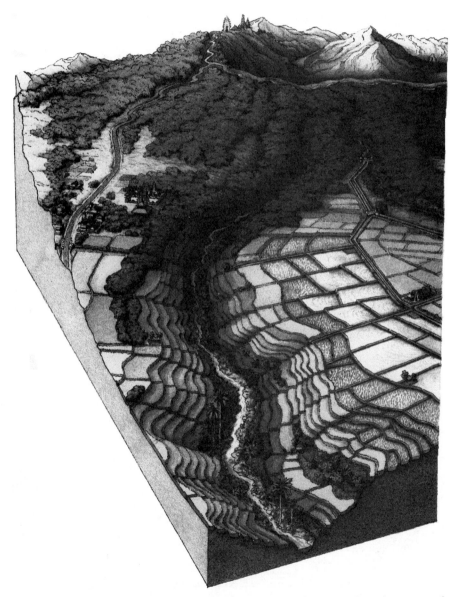

An artist's impression of the water temple system, showing the Temple of the Crater Lake on the crater rim of Mount Batur, and smaller subak temples adjoining the irrigation canals and rice terraces.

Plan of the Temple of the Crater Lake

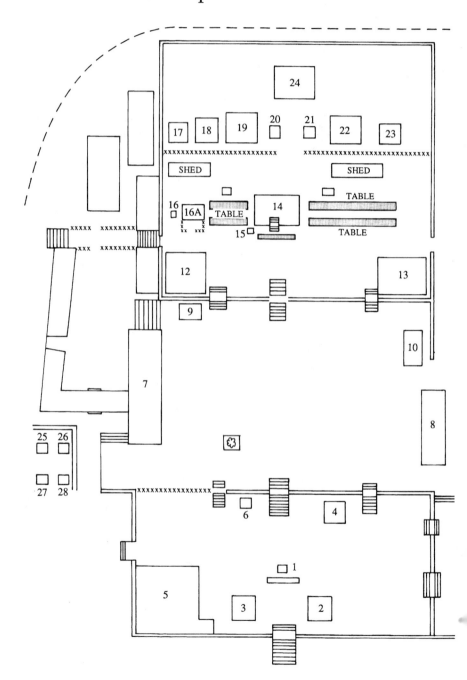

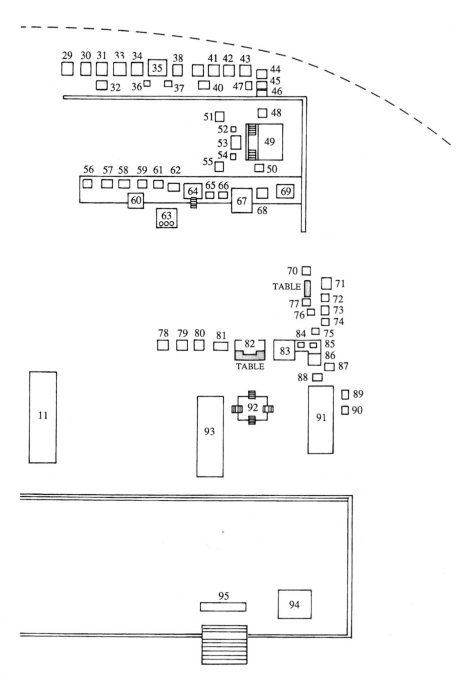

1. Anantabogha: Shrine for the World Serpent

2. Bale kulkul: Tower for drum

3. Bale kulkul: Tower for drum

4. Bale pekajah: Here one requests purification by holy water before entering the inner courtyards.

5. Bale Gong Gde: Orchestra pavilion for the fifty-piece Gong Gde orchestra

6. Kertamasa: Shrine for offerings keyed to Icaka months

7. Bale Pengeraosan: "Speech Pavilion," where guests are welcomed

8. Bale Gajah: Pavilion for priests and elders

9. Pesepilan: "Secrets" shrine

10. Bale Angklung: Pavilion for angklung orchestra

11. Dapur Suci: Temple kitchens and storerooms

12. Bale Badung: General-purpose pavilion named for the kingdom of Badung. Here the scribe receives delegations; priests and guests rest; offerings are readied for presentation at the main shrines; anthropologists take notes.

13. Bale Pemujan: "Pavilion for Worship," similar to No. 12

14. Peparuman Agung: Sacred storehouse for images of the gods and temple heirlooms

15. Jajan Gumi: Pedestal for the offering called Jajan Bumi, a cosmological symbol made of edible ingredients

    Tables: These permanent tables were recently installed to replace the temporary tables made of bamboo. Their purpose is to provide a place for offerings to the deities. Beneath the innermost row of tables, the priests store containers for holy water, and rest during the long rituals.

16. Pelinggih I Ratu Gde Subandar: Shrine for the "Great Lord Harbormaster," provisioner to the supreme gods. This shrine, and No. 16A, are supported and maintained by Balinese of Chinese descent.

16A. Peparuman Ratu Gde Subandar: Sacred storehouse for the "Great Lord Harbormaster," a god of money

17. Meru Tumpang 3: Three-storied meru shrine, associated with a deity of the district of Tejakula in north Bali

18. Meru Tumpang 5: Five-storied meru shrine for Bhatari Sakti Manik Astagina, a goddess associated with the ancestry of the former kingdom of Mengwi in south-central Bali

19. Meru Tumpang 9: Nine-storied meru shrine, for Ratu Gde Meduwe Gumi ("Great Lord who owns the Realm"), associated with the temple of Lempuyang

20. Pelinggih Penyarikan: Shrine for the Scribe (Penyarikan). The ambiguity of this name is intentional, for the shrine refers both to a divinized scribe who is the servant of the greater gods, and the human scribe of the temple.

21. Pelinggih Penyarikan: The hierarchy of temple priests includes two scribes, the Greater and the Lesser. Perhaps for this reason, there are also two of these shrines.

22. Meru Tumpang 9: Nine-storied meru shrine for Bhatara Gde Gunung Agung, the supreme deity of Mount Agung and of Besakih Temple

23. Meru Tumpang 5: Five-storied meru shrine for the deity of the former princedom of Blahbatuh

24. Meru Tumpang 11: The supreme shrine of the temple, with eleven stories, which is the maximum. This shrine is identified in two ways: either as the shrine of Dewi Danu, the Goddess of the Lake, or as the shrine for Bhatara Kalih Putranjaya. Bhatara Kalih Putranjaya means "The Two Gods of Putranjaya" or "The Dual God Putranjaya," the Goddess of the Lake and the God of Mount Agung. However, the goddess is supreme in this shrine, even when she is symbolically linked to the god.

25. Bebali courtyard: Middle courtyard of the main temple, usually used for performances by the Baris Gde and Rejang dancers, the Gong Gde orchestra, Topeng dancers, and other bebalian performances

26. Nawa-Sangha: During the Panca Wali Krama ceremonies of 1987, the nawa-sangha temporary offerings enclosure was situated here.

27. Wali: The innermost courtyard of the main temple

28. Temporary bale for Panca Wali Krama: Here the emblems and images (arca) of the deities were placed for blessings by Brahmana priests (pedanda) at the conclusion of Panca Wali Krama.

29–34: These six shrines form a group. The names of the deities worshipped in them are as follows:

29. Ratu Ayu Pecatu
30. Ratu Ayu Pinget
31. Ratu Ayu Kling
32. Ratu Ayu Shri Penpen
33. Ratu Ayu Kebek Sai
34. Ratu Ayu Teka Sai

The meaning of this collection of shrines (29–34) is suggested by the names of the deities. "Ratu" is a royal title, and "ayu" means "attractive," and has a feminine connotation. The meaning of the names of the goddesses is as follows:

"Pecatu" is a measure of rice. "Pingit" means sacred, and is described as the "sibling" of Pecatu. "Shri" means the Rice Goddess. "Kling" means utterance or command. "Penpen" means to keep or save. "Kebek sai" means always full, always present, and "teka sai" means always comes or comes every day.

The relationships among these deities are described in terms of a process. "After the command of Ratu Kling, the Rice Goddess retains the rice. The rice is saved in sacred (pinget) measures (pecatu); it always comes and the pecatu is always full (kebek sai)."

Shrine No. 35 is a three-storied meru shrine for the deity of the Pasek clans. All of the priests of the temple belong to one of the Pasek clans. The Greater Jero Gde belongs to the Paseks of the Black Wood (Kayu Selem), while the Lesser Jero Gde is a Pasek of Gelgel, the legendary southern kingdom. See Lansing (1991, p. 72–110) for interpretation.

35. I Ratu Gde Pasek (or Kepasekan)
36. pepelik (offerings shrine for No. 35)
37. pepelik (offerings shrine for No. 35)

The next set of shrines also form a group. The identities of the deities worshipped in the shrines are as follows:

38. Ratu Gde Manik Blabur
39. Ratu Gde Manik Melele
40. pepelik (offering shrine for No. 39 and No. 41)
41. Ratu Gde Manik Senjata
42. Ratu Gde Manik Malegadan
43. Ratu Ngurah Runcing

These shrines are often used by the metalsmiths (Pande clans). "Melele" means sharp; "Malegadan" means burnished or gleaming; "Senjata" means edged weapon and "Runcing" means sharp. "Blabur" means rain. Some informants suggest a link between rain and the cooling of metal after it has been forged; others insist that this shrine is not connected with the smith shrines directly. Rather, they say, it is a shrine where one may ask for rain.

44–47. no longer exist

48. Ratu Gde Perahu: The deity of boats. One informant suggested that this deity is a messenger who travels along waterways.

49. Meru Tumpang 3: Three-storied shrine for Ratu Mpu Dwijendra/Ratu Pura Jati; shrine to the divinized priest Mpu Dwijendra, linked to the origin of the lineage of the Greater Jero Gde, the Paseks of the Black Wood.

50. Ratu Magening: The deity of purification. This deity and the deity of No. 49 play an important role in the concept of a mandala of sacred waters supplying irrigation water to the subaks. On the floor of the crater near the lake, there is a subsidiary temple, called Pura Jati (No. 49, shrine of the principal deity). Beside the lake, there is a small shrine to Ratu Magening, where holy water is sought. It is said that Ratu Magening causes the waters of the lake to circulate, and so decides how much water will flow in a given direction. The main odalan (festival) at the Pura Jati occurs at the full moon of the first month, in the midst of the dry season, and is well-attended by the subaks.

51–55. offerings shrines and statues for No. 49

The following nine shrines form a group:

56. Ratu Sumampat
57. Ratu Bunut
58. Ratu Manukan
59. Ratu Ayu Mas Magelung
60. Ratu Ayu Tusan
61. Ratu Mas Sakti
62. Ratu Bangun Sakti
63. Ratu Ayu Kentel Gumi
64. Pesamuan No. 61–No. 63

Ratu Ayu Kentel Gumi, "Lord of the Thick Earth," is the ruler of this group. The first shrine in the row (No. 56) is used for offerings to control agricultural pests. "Bunut" is a type of tree. "Manuk" means bird. "Mas magelung" is a dancer's golden headdress. "Tusan" is the name of the legendary smith who created metalworking. "Mas sakti" means sacred gold. "Bangun sakti" means sacred building.

65. Ratu Pekiisan: "Pekiisan" comes from the word for a procession to seek holy water (mekiis). This deity provides holy water to candidates for priesthood at the temple.

66. Ratu Ayu Jelung

67. Ratu Gde Makolem: "Makolem" means sleep. Offerings for couples planning marriage are made here.

68. Ratu Gulem: "Gulem" means rain clouds.

69. Ratu Gde Baturrenggong

The remaining shrines (No. 70–No. 94) constitute a separate temple, the Pura Puseh Batur (Navel Temple of the Village of Batur). A single exception is No. 83, the drum tower, where a drum is struck forty-five times every morning, in honor of the forty-five principal deities of the temple.

78. Ida Iratu Dalem Majapahit
79. Ida Iratu Tambang Layar
80. Ida Iratu Gde Dalem Mesim
81. Ida Iratu Gde Dalem Mekah
82. Sanggar Agung: Surya, Chandra, Bayu
83. Bale kulkul tengeran Ida Bhatara
84. Pretiwi Ulun Bale Agung

85. divider

86. I Ratu Rambut Sedana

87. I Ratu Bhatari Cri

88. Pepelik Bhatari Cri

89. Ratu Paumbukang

90. pepelik

91. Bale Agung Bedanginan solas lobang

92. Bale Pesamuan Agung

93. Bale Agung Bedauhan siu lobang

94. Bale Perebuan

95. Apit lawang

Films about Bali

Bali is a favorite destination for documentary film crews, who create a never-ending stream of popular films about the island. This list describes my own personal view of the films that are likely to be most interesting to an anthropologist.

Films by Margaret Mead and Gregory Bateson in the Character Formation in Different Cultures *Series*

Trance and Dance in Bali, 1951, 20 minutes, 16mm, black and white
Distributor: New York University Film Library
   26 Washington Place
   New York, N.Y. 10003

A classic film that portrays the conflict between Rangda and Barong, described in Chapter 2 of this book. This film was reviewed by Hildred Geertz in the *American Anthropologist* (78:725–726, 1976).

A Balinese Family, 1951, 17 minutes, 16mm, black and white
Distributor: New York University Film Library
   26 Washington Place
   New York, N.Y. 10003

A study of a Balinese family showing the way in which father and mother treat the three youngest children—the lap baby, the knee baby, and the child nurse. There are scenes showing the father giving the baby his breast, the behavior of the knee baby during the lap baby's absence, and the difficulties the small-child nurse encounters in caring for the younger baby.

Films Distributed by Documentary Educational Resources
101 Morse St., Watertown, MA 02172
Tel. 617-926-0491 Fax 617-926-9519

The Three Worlds of Bali, 1980, 57 minutes, 2 reels, color
Produced and directed by Ira R. Abrams
Based on the research of J. Stephen Lansing

On the Indonesian island of Bali, the arts permeate almost every aspect of daily life. Gamelan music, wayang (shadow puppet) theater, dance, and elaborately constructed offerings of foods and flowers all represent attempts to please the gods and placate demons. In Balinese cosmology, demons are thought to dwell in the watery underworld, gods in the upper world, and human beings in the middle realm between the two. Much of human effort is directed towards maintaining the proper balance between these worlds, and between the forces of growth and decay.

The pinnacle of such efforts is the ritual Eka Dasa Rudra, held once every hundred years. The entire population of the island is mobilized for this event, preparing offerings and streaming from hundreds of village temples in processions to the sea. Eleven demons, of which Rudra is the most powerful, must be transformed into beneficent gods. No one who participated in the ritual filmed in 1979 had ever witnessed its performance, and so the ritual was based on writings in ancient lontar-palm-leaf manuscripts.

There is also a political dimension to Eka Dasa Rudra. In 1963, upon the urging of then president Sukarno, Balinese priests prepared to hold the ritual before the calendrically appropriate date. Preparations were followed by the first eruption in recorded history of Bali's great volcano, Gunung Agung. This terrible disaster was seen by many as a confirmation of the powers of the gods and demons, and of the necessity of performing the ritual correctly at the end of the Icaka century. In the spring of 1979, when Eka Dasa Rudra was finally held, the Indonesian president arrived, but not by helicopter, which, it was feared, might have annoyed the descending Rudras.

The Goddess and the Computer, 1988, 58 minutes, color video
Produced and directed by J. Stephen Lansing and André Singer

For centuries, rice farmers on the island of Bali have taken great care not to offend Dewi Danu, the water goddess who dwells in the crater lake near the peak of the Batur volcano. Toward the end of each rainy season, the farmers send representatives to Ulun Danu Batur, the temple at the top of the mountain, to offer pigs, ducks, coins, coconuts, and rice in thanks for the water that sustains their fields. Outsiders have long considered the rituals of Agama Tirtha, "the religion of holy water," an interesting but impractical way to grow crops. Development organizations have spent millions trying to improve on the ancient system.

With the help of an ingenious computer program, anthropologist Steve Lansing and ecologist James Kremer have shown that the Balinese rice growers have been practicing state-of-the-art resource management. Besides pleasing the goddess, it turns out, the island's ancient rituals serve to coordinate the irrigation and planting schedules of hundreds of scattered villages. And as the computer model makes clear, the result is one of the most stable and efficient farming systems on the planet.

The film depicts the water temples, the dams, and the development of the computer program at the University of Southern California. Viewers see the government officials call on the priests and begin to recognize the importance of their role. Viewers also see the power play as each group wants to control the use of the computer.

A Balinese Trance Seance, 1979, 30 minutes, 16 mm color film or video
Filmmakers: Timothy and Patsy Asch
Anthropologist: Linda Connor

Jero Tapakan, a spirit medium in a small, central Balinese village, consults with a group of clients in her household shrine. An introduction precedes the main seance, providing a visual impression of a seance and background information on the medium and her profession. The clients wish to contact the spirit of their dead son to discover the cause of his death and his wishes for his cremation ceremony. Jero is possessed several times in the course of the seance: first by a protective houseyard deity who demands propitiary offerings that had been previously overlooked; then by the spirit of the petitioner's dead father, who requests further offerings to ease his path in the other world; and finally by the spirit of the son. In an emotional scene, the son's spirit reveals the cause of his premature death (vengeful magic) and instructions for his forthcoming cremation. Between each trance, the medium converses with her clients, clarifying vague points in the often ambiguous trance speech.

The series of three films on Jero Tapakan are also the subject of a monograph: *Jero Tapakan: Balinese Healer,* by Linda Connor, Patsy Asch, and Timothy Asch (Cambridge: Cambridge University Press, 1986).

Jero on Jero: A Balinese Trance Seance Observed, 1980, 17 minutes, 16 mm color film or video
Filmmakers: Timothy and Patsy Asch
Anthropologist: Linda Connor

In 1980, anthropologist Linda Connor and filmmakers Tim and Patsy Asch returned to Bali with videocassette recordings of *A Balinese Trance Seance.* Jero Tapakan, the spirit medium, was invited to view the footage. The resulting film presents some of her reactions and her comments to Connor as she watched and listened to herself in trance. Jero had a unique opportunity to spontaneously and consciously react to and reflect upon the experience of possession. Her comments provide insights into how she feels while possessed, her understanding of witchcraft, and her humility in the presence of the supernatural world. More mundane thoughts are revealed as well— for example, the importance of the fine appearance of her house.

Jero on Jero could be most fruitfully viewed as a companion to *A Balinese Trance Seance,* which might be shown first and followed by a discussion, before screening Jero Tapakan's own response.

The Medium Is the Masseuse: A Balinese Massage, 1982, 35 minutes, 16 mm color film or video
Filmmakers: Timothy and Patsy Asch
Anthropologist: Linda Connor

Unlike many spirit mediums, Jero Tapakan practices as a masseuse once every three days, when possession is not auspicious. This film focuses on Jero's treatment of Ida Bagus, a member of the nobility from a neighboring town. Jero has been treating her client for sterility and seizures. She begins work this day with religious preparations and the assembling of traditional medicines. Treatment includes a thorough massage, administration of eye drops, an infusion, and a special paste for the chest. The dialogue, which is subtitled, includes a detailed discussion among anthropologist Linda Connor, Ida Bagus, and Jero about the nature and treatment of the illness, as well as informal banter among Jero, her other patients, and people in her houseyard. In an interview, Ida Bagus and his wife speak about the ten-year history of his illness and a variety of diagnoses. A broad view of Jero's practice is given in the film's conclusion, which shows excerpts from the treatments of other patients.

Glossary of Balinese Terms

Alangö: Old Javanese term for "beauty" or rapture
Asta Kosala Kosali: traditional architectural handbooks
Babad: court chronicle
Badoeng: before the Dutch conquest, a kingdom in southern Bali
Badung: a modern Balinese administrative district, roughly coterminous with the old kingdom of Badoeng
Banas Pati Rajah: leader of the four "birth spirits" *(kanda empat),* who also empowers the Barong
Barong: a mythological creature, whose sacred costume is usually stored in the village temple
Bebayi: evil spirits created by sorcery
Bedugul: a small rice-field shrine to agricultural deities
Bhuana agung: the macrocosm, variously interpreted to mean the universe, the visible world, or the island of Bali
Bhuana alit: the microcosm, or inner self of a human being
Bhur: the underworld
Brahmana (Brahman, Brahmin): a member of the highest-ranking Balinese descent groups, who may become high priests *(pedanda).* Often equated with the Indian Hindu concept of a Brahmin caste.
Bwah: the middle world of human beings
Calon Arang: the "candidate witch," a popular religious drama often performed in the Temple of Death *(Pura Dalem)*
Gamelan: a genre of Balinese music that includes metallophone instruments
Geguritan: a genre of Balinese poetry
Ida Ayu: the title of a female Brahmana
Ida Bagus: the title of a male Brahmana
Indra: king of the Gods
Jero Gde: "great sir," the name or title of the foremost priests of Batur temple
Kaja: the direction upstream or toward the mountains
Kanda empat: the four "birth spirits" or siblings of a human soul, whose leader is Banas Pati Rajah
Kakawin: Old Javanese poetry
Kelod: the direction downstream or toward the sea
Kidung: a genre of Balinese poetry
Ksatriya (see also Satriya): in Hindu philosophy, the warrior or ruling caste
Mahabharata: ancient Indian epic poem
Maya: illusion
Niskala: the unseen world
Odalan: Low Balinese term for a temple festival
Pamali: a sickness caused by witchcraft
Puputan: a fight to the death, from *puput* (ending)
Pura: temple
Puri: palace or nobleman's residence
Rangda: a Balinese witch, who opposes the Barong in various ritual performances. Rangda also means "widow."
Sakti: magically powerful

Sastra: literature

Satriya: in Hindu philosophy, the warrior or ruling caste

Sekala: the visible world

Siwa: one of the supreme Hindu deities worshipped by the Balinese

Sudra: in Hindu philosophy, the "commoner" caste

Taksu: a name for a household shrine believed to be visited by ancestral spirits; also may refer to trance possession or compelling dramatic performance

Tenget: magically dangerous

Tika: a Balinese calendar that depicts the interlocking weeks of the *uku,* from one to ten

Tirtha: holy water

Wesya: in Hindu philosophy, a caste of lesser nobles or merchants

Recommended Readings

Note: Listed below are a few of the many publications on Bali, all in English. For a comprehensive bibliography, see David J. Stuart-Fox, *Bibliography of Bali: Publications from 1920 to 1990*. Leiden: Koninklijk Instituut voor Taal-, Land- en Volkenkunde Bibliographical Series 19, 1992.

Bandem, I Made, and F.E. deBoer
1981 *Kaja and Kelod: Balinese Dance in Transition.* Kuala Lumpur: Oxford University Press.

Barth, Frederick
1993 *Balinese Worlds.* Chicago: University of Chicago Press.

Bateson, Gregory, and Margaret Mead
1942 *Balinese Character: A Photographic Analysis.* Special publications of the New York Academy of Sciences, vol. 2. New York.

Belo, Jane
1936 "A Study of the Balinese Family." *American Anthropologist* 38:12–31.

1949 "Bali: Rangda and Barong." *American Ethnological Society Monographs,* no. 16. Locust Valley, New York.

1970 (ed.) *Traditional Balinese Culture.* New York: Columbia University Press.

Boon, James A.
1977 *The Anthropological Romance of Bali, 1597–1972.* New York: Cambridge University Press.

Connor, Linda, Patsy Asch, and Timothy Asch
1986 *Jero Tapakan: Balinese Healer.* Cambridge: Cambridge University Press.

Covarrubias, Miguel
1973 [1937] *Island of Bali.* New York: Knopf.

Creese, Helen
1991 "Balinese Babad as Historical Sources: A Reinterpretation of the Fall of Gelgel." Leiden: *Bijdragen tot de Taal-, Land- en Volkenkunde* 147: 236–260.

Eiseman, Fred B., Jr.
1989 *Bali: Sekala and Niskala* (2 vols.). Berkeley and Singapore: Periplus Editions.

Geertz, Clifford
1959 "Form and Variation in Balinese Village Structure." *American Anthropologist* 61:991–1012.

1973 *The Interpretation of Cultures*. New York: Basic Books.

1980 *Negara: The Balinese Theatre State in the Nineteenth Century*. Princeton: Princeton University Press.

Geertz, Hildred
1991 (ed.) *State and Society in Bali*. Leiden, The Netherlands: KITLV Press.

1994 *Images of Power: Balinese Paintings Made for Margaret Mead and Gregory Bateson*. Honolulu: University of Hawaii Press.

Geertz, Hildred, and Clifford Geertz
1975 *Kinship in Bali*. Chicago: University of Chicago Press.

Guermonprez, Jean-Francois
1989 "Dual Sovereignty in Nineteenth Century Bali." *History and Anthropology* 4:189–207.

Hobart, Mark, and R.H. Taylor
1986 *Context, Meaning and Power in Southeast Asia*. Ithaca, New York: Cornell Southeast Asia Program.

Hooykaas, Christiaan
1964 *Agama Tirtha: Five Studies in Hindu-Balinese Religion*. Amsterdam: Noord-Hollandsche Uitgevers Maatschappij.

1973 *Religion in Bali*. Leiden: Brill.

Howe, L.E.A.
1984 "Gods, People, Spirits and Witches: The Balinese System of Person Definition." Leiden: *Bijdragen tot de Taal-, Land- en Volkenkunde* 140: 193–222.

Lansing, J. Stephen
1974 *Evil in the Morning of the World: Phenomenological Approaches to a Balinese Community*. Ann Arbor: Michigan Papers on South and Southeast Asia, No. 6.

1983 *The Three Worlds of Bali*. New York: Praeger.

1987 "Balinese Water Temples and the Management of Irrigation," *American Anthropologist* 89(2): 326–341.

1991 *Priests and Programmers: Technologies of Power in the Engineered Landscape of Bali*. Princeton, N.J.: Princeton University Press.

Lansing, J. Stephen, and James N. Kremer
1993 "Emergent Properties of Balinese Water Temple Networks: Coadaptation on a Rugged Fitness Landscape." *American Anthropologist* 95(1): 97–114.

McPhee, Colin
1986 [1946] *A House in Bali.* Singapore: Oxford University Press.

Mershon, Katharane E.
1971 *Seven Plus Seven, Mysterious Life-Rituals in Bali.* New York: Vantage Press.

Ramseyer, Urs
1977 *The Art and Culture of Bali.* Oxford: Oxford University Press.

Schulte Nordholt, H.
1986 *Bali: Colonial Conceptions and Political Change 1700–1940: From Shifting Hierarchies to 'Fixed' Order.* Rotterdam: Comparative Asian Studies Programme 15, Erasmus University.

Suryani, Luh Ketut, and Gordon Jensen
1993 *Trance and Possession in Bali.* Oxford: Oxford University Press.

Swellengrebel, J.L.
1960 (ed.) *Bali: Life, Thought and Ritual.* The Hague: W. van Hoeve.

1969 (ed.) *Bali: Further Studies in Life, Thought and Ritual.* The Hague: W. van Hoeve.

Vickers, Adrian
1989 *Bali, A Paradise Created.* Berkeley and Singapore: Periplus Editions.

Warren, Carol
n.d. *Adat and Dinas: Balinese Villages in the Indonesian State.* Singapore: Oxford University Press.

Worsley, Peter J.
1972 *Babad Buleleng: A Balinese Dynastic Geneaology.* The Hague: Nijhoff.

Zoete, Beryl de, and Walter Spies
1973 [1938] *Dance and Drama in Bali.* Kuala Lumpur: Oxford University Press.

Zoetmulder, P.J.
1974 *Kalangwan: A Survey of Old Javanese Literature.* The Hague: M. Nijhoff.

Zurbuchen, Mary
1987 *The Language of the Balinese Shadow Theatre.* Princeton, N.J.: Princeton University Press.

INDEX